MW01615677

hhhhhh
2018

Scrambled Wisdom

Almost isn't is ... is it

All poems written by Baxter Black
Copyright © 2017 by Baxter Black

Published by: Coyote Cowboy Company
PO Box 2190
Benson, AZ 85602
All rights reserved
Cover and book design by Becky Harvey

LIBRARY OF CONGRESS CATALOGING IN PUBLICATION DATA
Main entry under:
Cowboy Poetry

Bibliography: p
1. Scrambled Wisdom: Almost isn't is, is it
2. Cowboy-Poetry
3. Poetry-Cowboy
4. Humor-Cowboy
5. Agriculture-Poetic Comment

I. Black, Baxter, 1945-

Library of Congress 2017944261
ISBN: 978-0-939343-64-5

OTHER BOOKS BY BAXTER
The Cowboy and His Dog
A Rider, A Roper And A Heck'uva Windmill Man
Doc, While Yer Here
Coyote Cowboy Poetry
Croutons On A Cow Pie
Cowboy Standard Time
Croutons On A Cow Pie, Vol 2
Hey, Cowboy, Wanna Get Lucky? *(Crown Publishing, Inc.)*
Dunny And The Duck
Cow Attack
Cactus Tracks And Cowboy Philosophy *(Crown Publishing, Inc.)*
A Cowful Of Cowboy Poetry
Horseshoes, Cowsocks And Duckfeet *(Crown Publishing, Inc.)*
Hey, Cowgirl, Need A Ride? *(Crown Publishing, Inc.)*
Blazin' Bloats & Cows On FIRE!
The World According to Baxter Black: Quips, Quirks, & Quotes
The Back Page *(Western Horseman Books)*
Lessons From A Desperado Poet *(TwoDot)*
Ride, Cowboy, Ride! 8 Seconds Ain't That Long *(TwoDot)*
Poems Worth Saving
Cave Wall Graffiti from a Neanderthal Cowboy
Tinsel, Mistletoe & Reindeer Bait

baxterblack.com

TABLE OF CONTENTS

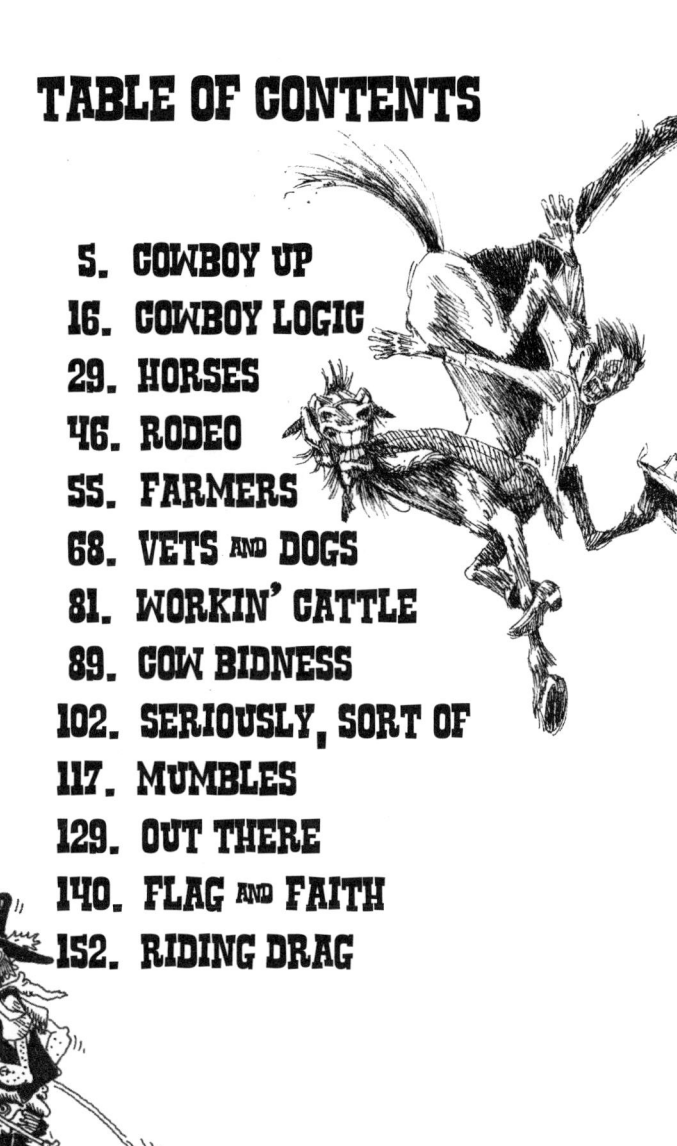

5. COWBOY UP

16. COWBOY LOGIC

29. HORSES

46. RODEO

55. FARMERS

68. VETS AND DOGS

81. WORKIN' CATTLE

89. COW BIDNESS

102. SERIOUSLY, SORT OF

117. MUMBLES

129. OUT THERE

140. FLAG AND FAITH

152. RIDING DRAG

DEDICATION

This book is dedicated to Pat Richardson; Dakota born, cowboy raised, California fed, and undoubtedly the funniest cowboy poet I've ever heard. He was droll, with a monotone delivery and every time you'd take a breath he'd drop a knee-slappin', dog barkin', rarin' back, stomp on the floor till the possum is dead "one liner" . . . that brought the house down!

When you feasted on Pat's plate, you didn't need an expert or a wall of plaques to know you were hearing a master of his art, making you laugh! Who else would write a poem called "The Donner Party Reunion."

I'm going to sprinkle him occasionally in this book with permission of his family. As Bob Edwards said about Mark Twain, he was great, because he was funny.

Crackin' 'em up at the Cowboy Poetry Gathering.

Photo by Jessica Lifland

Cowboy Up

ON THE BRONC TO BREAKFAST

"Bronc to Breakfast" is my favorite Charlie Russell painting.

In the world of cowboys, if you survive one of those "feelin' frisky" bucking horse mornings you can earn a little cowboy cred . . . whether you ride him or not!

Jim jumped on his good horse and touched him lightly with a spur. In the time it took for him to think 'did I pull the cinch tight?' the ten year old gelding fired him over the fence and into the machinery shed!

The hospital stay was humiliating enough but he never got over what his cowboy friends saw when they looked at the records posted on the end of his bed. They all saw his diagnosis: FELL OFF HIS HORSE.

AFTERTHOUGHT
People will always remember your faux pas, it's like breaking wind at a funeral.

ON HOW'DYA HURT YER NOSE?

I got cracked across the bridge. Not that my nose needs any more attention. As one friend put it, "Bax, if you'd lie down on your back in the sun, we could tell time!"

I knew I'd be asked what happened. I could have said, "I was swatting flies with the branding iron!" But that answer seemed so mundane.

"I was riding night herd when the cattle stampeded! I dove off my horse to save a small baby calf. I buried us to keep from being run over, noses up! Unfortunately the calf died but South Dakota is planning a monument in the shape of my nose beside Crazy Horse, to commemorate allergies everywhere."

The sign says,
NO PICKING ALLOWED.

AFTERTHOUGHT
Protruding prehensile proboscis?
Probably pretty presumptuous, I'd say.

7

ON A LETTER FROM ALF

Alf came to rope at our branding. Unfortunately he had lost his 60' rope in the gather. I lent him mine.

Alf missed the first three. Then he dropped his rope and stayed on the ground. Finally after seven more attempts, he caught one!

He made a quick wrap around his waist and braced himself. The calf was doing 35 mph when the slack ran out. To our amazement, after a sled run around the corral, the calf tangled in the line and crashed! We tied the calf down and, the whole crew gave Alf a big round of applause!

During supper the story was told over and over. He leaned over and said, "I told ya I could do it."

And though he was past his prime all of us agreed, "By gosh, he's still got what it takes!"

AFTERTHOUGHT
"He's a nice feller, but he'll bear watchin'." - Elmer Kelton

ON THE CACTUS PHOTO

I was snapping away and stepped back. My spurs hit an obstacle and I sat, backside first... into the welcoming arms of prickly pear maximus as big as a Barcalounger!

After the requisite signal, "Ay-y-y-y-y-y-y-y-y!" I checked the damage. It came loose like Velcro.

Pulling myself back together, so to speak, I climbed back on my horse. Eventually I adopted a sort of horizontal straddle with my right boot still in the stirrup, my head between his ears and my left hip glaring like a solar panel toward the sun!

I still live in fear that some spy satellite photo is now classified as an infiltrator disguised as a sunbathing acrobat!

AFTERTHOUGHT

A cowboy without a horse is like a bird without wings. A cowboy without wings is like a bow leg-ged ostrich!

ON THE WAY A COWBOY FEELS

Oh Lord, you gave this ranch to me.

I don't own a stick of it, but it's mine.

Every ledge, edge, hedge, boulder, rock and stone.

I know the highest point in each pasture.

I know which calf goes with which cow.

I'm the only one who can start the water truck when it freezes.

I know how many 400 lb calves fit in a 20' trailer.

I know the combination to every lock on the place.

I don't drink enough water.

I wear out my boot soles but not the heels.

My gloves last about 3 months if I don't lose them.

I know which horse to trust and which one to watch.

I can braid, rivet, hammer, shape, tape, tear, shoe, clip, cut, bob, whistle, dig, tip, snip, snap, and call the welder when I need to.

My hat holds water.

AFTERTHOUGHT

...I'm indispensible...and I'm the first one they let go when the ranch changes hands.

ON COW STUPIDITY

Will's dad told him, "Cows are stupid, that's why we eat them."

Is it stupidity when you try to run a range bull through a chute three days in a row and he resists? A cow can hide her calf, walk half a mile to water then return to the it's hiding place. Instinct or intelligence?

Maybe stupid is too harsh a word. We could say Learning Impaired, IQ Diminished, Thinking Deprived, Brain Dead. And Stupid compared to what? A creosote post, a box of gravel, a tamping bar?

To be fair to the cows we must look at the company they keep...other cows, and of course, cowboys...who aren't stupid but sometimes you can't tell.

AFTERTHOUGHT
A penny for your thoughts. Make it two thoughts if you can't make change.

ON ONLINE DATING RURALMATE.FEM

FarmersOnly.com is a successful dating service that finds compatible couples with rural roots. I'm certain they must set some standard to sort off the ringers.

But in our mythical RURALMATE.FEM there are no restrictions.

NORWEIGIAN BACHELORS and WEST TEXAS RANCHERS *of a certain age:*

Lonely? Desolate? Starved out? Companion available: Over 30 years old, can dead-lift 200 lbs, has been vaccinated for tetanus, flu, shingles, BSE, Bangs, Anaplaz and Nile virus. Can make biscuits out of creosote bush, sagebrush and leafy spurge, still knickers and is playful, is a dead-shot and is willing to move.

ON THE HUMAN ATTACHMENT PROLAPSE

The cow lay on her belly straining, tiny hooves peeking from beneath her tail. Steffan draped OB chains over each of his wrists and calf's feet and pulled back.

It startled the cow. She rose in a fit of bewilderment and took off!

Stuck like a rock in David's slingshot, Steffan's lower extremities pounded and pummeled the rocks, posts and frozen mud. With one solid collision into an old feeder, he gathered enough slack to fly free of the chains!

Thinking she had calved, the cow began to lick him clean. "Is that all?" I asked Steffen.

"Yes," he said, but somewhere in the back of his mind he remembered getting to his knees and trying to nurse.

AFTERTHOUGHT
"Got Milk?"

ON PAT RICHARDSON'S ACCUMULATIONS

 "Did you get *that* job? Sounds like it was just up your alley?"

"No. I talked to the human resources and she asked to see my testamonials."

"Well, surely you had some?"

"Ya know, if I'd had a better education, I'd probably still have that job."

 The only thing that Hillary and Donald share is the right to a jury trial.

 He couldn't afford the operation so his doctor touched up his X-Rays.

 I'm not intelligent enough to have a solution, I'm barely smart enough to admire the problem.

 I asked the dentist why he's wearing earplugs. He said he was out of Novacaine.

ON COWBOY COFFEE

The barista took my order and commented that he didn't know that cowboys drank Starbucks. I said, "We invented it!"

As I explained it to him, just put a handful of coffee grounds in an ol' pot, put it on an open fire and set it on "boil!"

The pot itself is sacred and never washed. It is seasoned by the remnants of whatever falls into the pot. It is not unlike a good pipe whose bowl get layered with carcinogenic ash, or the wax that builds in your ears, or the plaque that barnacles an ol' dog's teeth.

Starbucks proudly touts its flavor, but if you really crave a strong, rank, acidic, caffeine stimulant, one that can also peel the paint off a backhoe bucket, penetrate zirconium nuclear rods, and destroy the odor in your son's tennis shoes, have an ol' cowboy make you a cuppa in his blackened pot. You will discover Starbuck's secret.

A WORD OF CAUTION:
If you can't strain your cowboy coffee through a two-inch ten gauge expanded metal ... at least drop a magnet into the cup before you sip!

Cowboy

LOGIC

THINGS AREN'T WHAT THEY SEEM TO BE

If you see an Indian dressed like a cowboy,
he's probably a cowboy.

If you see a cowboy dressed like an Indian,
he's probably a country singer.

If you see an Indian dressed like an Indian,
he's probably an entertainer.

If you see a salesman dressed like a cowboy,
he's probably a realtor.

If you see a golfer dressed like a farmer,
he's probably a salesman.

If you see a farmer dressed like a salesman,
he's probably a golfer.

If you see a farmer dressed like a cowboy,
he's probably on vacation.

If you see a lawman dressed like a cowboy,
he's probably the sheriff.

If you see a cowboy dressed like a lawman,
likely you're in Wyoming or Georgia.

If you see a sheriff in the rear view mirror,
you're probably in trouble.

If you see a movie star dressed like a cowboy,
he's probably Hopalong Cassidy.

If you see Hoppy in short pants,
he's probably at a Celebrity Golf Tournament.

If you see a cowboy dressed like Hoppy,
he's probably a cowboy poet.

IT'S A WONDER YOU WEREN'T KILLED!

"Well, all I did was rope that sorry, no good, fightin' bull then tie him to a post...I must have had too much slack in the line...or underestimated my body length...kept tryin' to hook me...still hangin' on to his tail...plum off the ground... we're both gettin' tangled in the rope...slung me high enough...sailed over...hit the...lucky though...just missed the windmill tool box...I coulda' been hurt!"

"It could'a been worse, I guess, if I hadn't come loose when he jumped the cattle guard!"

AFTERTHOUGHT

*"Knocked me out.
Thank goodness I
was wearin' my hat!"*

ON WHY THE NORTH STAR IS SO HUMBLE

It has the most important job in our northern hemisphere. Some say Orion or the Scorpio rule the night sky. They come on the stage every night and give a spectacular performance, but then they take a bow and leave! Plus, they take long vacations!

The Big Dipper is useful. His job is to point. But he too might disappear below the night horizon. Takin' a break, I guess.

That leaves Ursa Minor, Polaris (alias the North Star), standing, immoveable, modestly doing its job. It is the flag pole of the planet, always there to help you find your way home. Not the brightest, but always enough to see the yard light on a farm in Union Center, South Dakota.

It doesn't have time to show off.

AFTERTHOUGHT
What is the difference between astronomy and astrology? Think medical doctor and chiropractor or non-fiction and fiction or physiology and philosophy.

ON CARPOOLING THE COWBOY WAY

Brett loaded his broke-down little hatchback into the stock trailer by rolling it down a hill and using ramps. "Great!" he thought...then tried to open the door...uh oh, too tight.

"No, sweat," he said as he tried to open the hatch. It was locked. The sides of the trailer were solid.

For 45 minutes he tried to get the attention of passers by. He whistled, banged on the trailer, and rocked the little car. Finally by plastering himself against the hatchback window and flailing like a shipwrecked sailor, he caught the attention of a bicycling journalism major.

She agreed to go get help if Brett agreed to let her film his plight and do an interview first. He was cornered and acquiesced. The article was titled, "Carpooling, the Cowboy Way!"

AFTERTHOUGHT
"God gave us shin bones so we could find trailer hitches in the dark."- Earl Dibbles, Jr.

ON THE MOTHER OF INVENTION

Uncle Jack needed to treat one of his bulls for pink eye from a moving pickup. He put together an injector that involved a plastic syringe, PVC pipe and lots of duct tape.

Rachel was driving and James was coaching as Uncle Jack leaned out of the pickup bed shouting directions!

With the coolness of Captain Ahab harpooning the White Whale, Jack drove home his injector javelin!

With the quickness of a maddened rhino, the blind bull pivoted perpendicular to the pickup, tore off the side mirror and jerked Uncle Jack overboard!

EPILOGUE
I asked James after he told me the story,
"Was the mirror the only thing he broke?"

"No," said James, "but that was the one thing we fixed!"

21

ON LOADING BULLS THE COWGIRL WAY

When Kristy's ol' cow came in heat she'd usually borrow one of her neighbor Tom's bulls.

"It's too muddy," Tom said. "If I caught one can I use him?" she asked. "Well I guess so." he said. The cowboys had a good laugh.

In less than an hour she pulled up in front of the café with a big Charlois bull in the back of her trailer. The Café crowd didn't believe it!

She had unloaded the haltered cow in a bull pasture and walked it up and down the edge.

Six bulls started slogging through the mud in her direction; something in the air, I guess! Kristy quickly reloaded the cow in the front of the trailer and shut the sorting gate. The first bull never hesitated, Kristy slammed the end gate on him, then drove back to the café.

Recess was called and the entire Coffee Shop Communion went out to inspect. "How did...?" Tom began. She never told 'em.

AFTERTHOUGHT

Lesson #30: When Superman says he's got the cards, don't bet against him.

22

ON STRONG WORDS

We took a tour on the new ranch. The new owner, John wanted to go clear to the top. We jumped in the new SUV. I threw my stuff in the back.

"Gun it!" John directed Roger, "Let's see some country!"

We ascended into the hills on a slick muddy track and finally reached the top. "We made it!" said John. "We have a flat tire!" said Roger.

The right front tire, big as a 757 jet intake was flat, leaving less than six inches of clearance between the axle and the saturated earth. I dug a hole to accommodate the eight-inch jack. As we turned the crank, the jack sunk out of sight.

"We need something flat and hard," announced John. "How strong are your words?"

I thought he was referring my colorful language but, he pointed to my box of the 224-page, hot off the press, brilliantly illustrated, brand new books!

It took four books to allow the jack to raise the 3 ton Excursion high enough to apply the spare.

"Strong words," said John as I scraped baseball-sized chunks of mud off my clothes and precious misshapen poetic volumes, "I'm sure glad it came out in the hardback!"

ON CHERRY BOMBS IN WINTER

As ranch kids, Sparky and his brother chased elk off the haystacks with snowmobiles and cherry bombs! They carried them in their shirt pockets and were allowed cigars as a punk to relight.

Years later, when Sparky had taken over the ranch, he was driving home one winter night and saw elk in the haystack.

He lit the cherry bombs, leaned out of the window and tossed them on the road. 'Super,' he thought, then he heard the hissing!

He looked down to see one of the cherry bombs nestled between his legs jubilantly throwing sparks like the 4th of July!

All Sparky would say about the damage was, it blew a hole in the seat cover!

 **AFTERTHOUGHT**
Their mother toilet trained them at gunpoint!
- Pat Richardson

24

ON BLACK CATTLE AND WHITE BEARS

'What is the logic in breeding heat-resistant cattle, then making them black?' wondered Stevo. Marketing, of course, but...what about the polar bear? Why are they white? They should be black to absorb the sun's rays in the frigid North.

The Arctic is said to be warming up. Polar bears are migrating south where their white hide can reflect the equatorial sun. Nature is finally making sense.

They are imitating the centuries old instinct of migrating snowbird farmers and team ropers who flock to Brawley, Yuma and McAllen every winter, where all the RV parks are packed full with 3⁄4 ton pickups and guess what...they are all WHITE!

AFTERTHOUGHT
People who wonder if the glass is half full or half empty miss the point. The glass is refillable. - Bill Geary

ON PELLETS VS. PILES

Why do cows make pies instead of pellets? If they did make pellets would they be large as an elk's...or larger? Baseball size? It would be dangerous to walk behind them. Dairymen would constantly be bonked on the head by a fecal projectile!

The admitting-room nurse would write down CBC (cow biscuit concussion) and ask about his insurance. At least with a cow pie you can get good coverage.

AFTERTHOUGHT
What is the purpose of a dew claw? To measure the dew?

ON THE RABBIT BRUSH

I was makin' a circle and spooked a big jack-rabbit from under a growth of Rabbit Brush. For the first time I actually thought, 'So, that's why they named it Rabbit Brush!'

I got to thinkin', what if the first pioneer had spooked a spider out of the brush, or an ant or a beer can? Think about it...Budweiser Brush! If underneath the brush there was a mouse mandible, you could call it Tooth Brush! Or if a wig jumped out it would be a Hair Brush, which would be redundant, of course, it is already named Hare Brush.

AFTERTHOUGHT
I'm glad nobody remembered the dung beetle...it might take the shine off my spurs!

ON COWBOY ADVICE TO THE LOVELORN NO.1

Dear Mr. Cowboy,

I've just fallen in love with a 38 year old bottle blonde who shoots a mean game of snooker and can chug a 16 oz bottle of Red Dog Ale in 30 seconds! Do you believe in love at first sight? Or should I wait till tomorrow morning to pop the question?

From Thunderstruck, texting in the men's room @ Walter's Crescendo Lounge

DEAR THUNDERSTRUCK,
Ask her quick before the Butazolidin and Acepromazine wear off and she realizes how stupid you are.

Dear Mr. Cowboy,

I met a woman in Sturgis at the Rally. She has a motorcycle and a tattoo. We're getting serious, but I don't want to play second fiddle to her cycle passion. Is she a good bet?

Signed, Idling In Idaho

DEAR IDS,
It depends. Is it a Harley . . . the tattoo, I mean?

28

Horses

ON THE HORSE SCULPTOR

I wonder if he starts at the head? Or starts at the hooves instead, one leg at a time, molding, making the limb yield to him till it feels just right.

Then does he go to the head? The facial expression will be a clue for what to expect from those powerful limbs that drive the beast through the picture in his mind. Will he break and run? Will the sculptor have to start again from the broken pieces?

All these Charlie Russell thoughts went through my mind as I watched the horse trainer sculpting a new horse from the muscle and bone that stood before him in the arena now.

Hide and hair, or clay and wire? Ray Hunt or Fredrick Remington? The casting and creation of a horse requires an eye for deception, a hand for communication, and a deep knowledge of what it takes to mold imagination into flesh and blood.

AFTERTHOUGHT
It also helps if you can give them a down payment...both artist or trainer...not too much, just enough to keep them hungry.

ON THE GIFT HORSE

Dave Holl says he's got the dumbest horse he ever tried to train. Named him Dumbo.

"I took him in the round pen to familiarize him with a rope. I accidentally hit him on the rump. He tripped over himself, fell against the rails and dumped me off!

"He's never learned to walk a straight line or follow a trail . . . jiggin' and trottin' from side to side. Absolutely worthless in the sorting alley, maybe because he's scared of cows."

"Surely he must have some good points?" I said.

"Yeah," said Dave, "For one, he's easy to catch. But then you have to ask yourself, 'What's the point?'"

AFTERTHOUGHT

A header often has two horses, his favorite and one in training. The heeler has one horse, in training and for sale.

31

ON FIRE BREATHING DRAGON

CB and Dale, his neighbor, found a dead chicken in the barnyard. "Feed it to the dogs, maybe pluck it first." said CB.

"How 'bout just singe them off?" asked Dale.

They put the corpse in an ol' paper sack, threw it in the horse pen and set it on fire. They were choring when they heard a huge ruckus!

They hurried back to the barn and saw the stud running through the flock with a big ball of fire in his mouth! He snorted and dropped a chicken foot. His whiskers and eyelashes were singed.

Our two wise men looked at each other. "Horses don't eat meat," said CB.

"Of course, they don't," said the 2nd wise man. At this, the fire-breathing dragon dropped his head and ate the foot.

AFTERTHOUGHT
Thank goodness horses cannot vomit.

ON THE FARRIER FAN CLUB

Shawn pulled the old shoe off Skeeter's left-front. He picked up his nippers and went to work. I can almost hear him humming a tune.

When suddenly...HE WOKE UP!

He was under the hitch rail! The shoeing box was broken, the foot rest overturned and he had a knot on his head the size of a lamb's kidney!

Skeeter stood warily six feet away with the broken halter snap hanging off his chin. Two sets of claw marks coursed from his rump like ski trails.

Salvo, the barn cat, was sitting in the windowsill licking his paw. Shawn studied him and he continued licking. "Don't ask me," he mewed, "I didn't see a thing."

AFTERTHOUGHT

I shoe my horse. I don't shoe other peoples. Most folks can't have them lame that long.

ON HORSES GOOD AS GOLD

Cheryl is the kind of woman that has little interest in learning more than the basics of horsemanship.

She climbed aboard trusty ol' Cannonball and settled in on husband Howard's squeakin' new saddle.

In the pen she approached a cow and leaned off the right side to read the tag. The saddle slipped and she was under Cannonball's belly with one foot still hung in the stirrup and completely upside down!

Howard found her later in the barn. His saddle was in three piles completely disassembled; unbuckled, unsnapped, untied, unwrapped and drug through mud.

After he heard her story he said, "My gosh! Why didn't you check the cinch?"

She plopped her hands on her hips and said indignantly, "Now who in the world would ever think of that?"

AFTERTHOUGHT
Some need a saddle with dashboard warning lights. Like "bit ajar", " breast collar crooked", or "loose cinch".

34

ON HORSE OWNER TIPS

It's fair to say that horses often become burdens to the owner. If you paid less than $2000, buying a new one is better than trying to live with an unsuitable one.

1) Horses are not people. You owe them nothing except a decent home and good treatment.

2) If a horse has a bad habit that you can live with, just let him do it and don't worry. If his bad habit is dangerous get rid of him fast as you can.

3) If your horse develops a chronic medical condition that interferes with SOUNDNESS, sell him. If it is only a BLEMISH keep him.

4) Do not believe everything the seller tells you. In the art of horse-trading, anything is legal! It's a game.

5) When a horse has served your purpose, take him to the nearest horse auction. You have no reason to feel guilty. Otherwise call a vet for euthanasia. Then you've got to bury him.

AFTERTHOUGHT
If you think your horse is a pet then ignore everything that I have said previously.

ON PRITCHELL ME!

I use what I call a "punch" to enlarge the nail holes on horseshoes. The tool's official name is "pritchell". They can be dangerous. A shoer told me that once while he was heating up his pritchell to reshape the tip with a hammer, the pritchell slipped from his grip. It spun upwards and the sharp, hot end went up his right nostril! He said he could hear it hiss as it cauterized his membranes!

AFTERTHOUGHT
I had a friend who was tightening a hose clamp on a slick pipe and stuck a screwdriver up his nose. I don't know if it was a standard or a phillips head?

ON ROASTING CHESTNUTS

I've always felt that the equine chestnut was overlooked. It is the vestigial remnant of prehistoric digits.

It is common knowledge that obscure lamenesses in horses are usually blamed on the shoer. But might it be a dislocated chestnut? Maybe that's why Napoleon really lost at Waterloo.

The song, "Chestnuts roasting on an open fire..." has been mistranslated down through the millennia. It is really derived from an old chant of the Senior Pro Rodeo Assn... "stressed nuts roping 'cause they can't retire..."

I have my own lucky chestnut. I take it with me every time I go riding. My horse carries it for me, plus a spare.

AFTERTHOUGHT
Not to mention the ergot, or did you say Uvula?

ON DONKEY DRESSAGE

Rob, a Virginia farmer, thrilled the world of burros when he conceived Donkey Dressage. It is a performance to allow the donkey on display to portray his true secret of long life, and the key...PACE YOURSELF!

So rather than leap over jumps at a high-lope, you accrue points by walking through them at a comfortable pace pushing the horizontal poles over and walking around water traps.

The objective is to do everything wrong!

Donkey basketball has been popular, now imagine Donkey bulldogging! But...instead of steers, they would use something more suited for the donkey attitude. How 'bout tortoise dogging! Obviously, it wouldn't be a timed event.

AFTERTHOUGHT
There is a place for Donkey Dressage . . . Mardi Gras!

ON ALFALFA VS. GRASS HAY FOR HORSES

Mature horses require 8-10% protein.

Average alfalfa hay is 16% protein. No protein supplement is required, although a block of mineral salt is a good addition.

Average meadow hay is 7-9% protein. A protein supplement like grain or molasses is probably needed with grass hay. Most people feed grass hay as a low nutrient fiber because their horses get fat from lack of exercise.

We have a huge industry that offers hundreds of choices for the horse owner. Many are professionally formulated for all kinds of specific purposes; horses that perform, be it team roping, reining, endurance competitors, race horses, et. al. There are also hundreds of choices of "alternative concoctions" that have never been proven to do anything and depend on the testimony of Uncle Horace who said it really works! Caveat emptor.

Personally I have owned and fed 60 or 70 horses over many years. I have always fed nothing but alfalfa.

AFTERTHOUGHT

I am not a professional nutritionist, but then again, neither is Uncle Horace.

ON EQUINE CHIROPRACTORY

Cowboy Dave Holl got bucked out of his Birkenstocks! He found himself on the ground and hip locked.

Riding was impossible. A couple days later Uncle Herman asked him to shoe his big Belgian mare.

Cowboy Dave had gotten around to the offside hind leg when the big mare began leaning her huge haunch on Dave's back, crushing him. He slowly collapsed as she slid along his back. He said he heard three little clicks, like a grandfather clock's Tick-Tock-Tick. He crumpled and rolled, then, without thinking he rose and stepped away...cured!

Hey, I believed him. I've heard of Equine Chiropractory, but not in that context.

In conclusion Dave answered the classic question, "Is there a doctor in the horse?!"

AFTERTHOUGHT
They say animal behavior can warn you when an earthquake is coming ... like the night before the last earthquake hit, our family dog took the car keys and drove to Arizona - Pat Richardson

ON NEW HORSES, ROUGH COUNTRY

Shorty was pushing a bull down a steep zig zag trail, ridin' a green gelding called Grullo. Somehow the bull turned and started comin' back up! Shorty went to hee-hawin' and hollerin' which spooked the young horse who jumped the bank and landed a'straddle of the bull!

In a panic the colt climbed back up the bank and took off draggin' Shorty's best saddle! When Shorty finally topped the rim there was the colt...shaking and in shock!

Not having any experience in his young life to compare to this, the colt actually walked up to Shorty, who touched the side of his face. Grullo sighed. I guess he just needed a hug.

AFTERTHOUGHT

Dave Stamey is also an outfitter who recommends a peanut butter sandwich for the saddlebag. It looks the same when you start up the trail or find it two days later.

ON CLAIMING TO BE A HORSESHOER

I never claimed to be a horseshoer and I've got the scars to prove it!

A permanent stoop, calluses and a slice across the inside of my thigh. I'd driven a #5 city head into the second hole of a size #1 shoe and the hoof wall on a skittish sorrel gelding when, just before I twisted the protruding nail, a disoriented fruit bat soared down out of the rafters and tangled in the horse's forelock!

He went bumfangled and jerked his foot out of my grip between my knees!

The wound has crudely healed, my girlfriend made a pair of cut-offs from my jeans, and we made a pair of coasters from the scraps of my shoeing apron.

AFTERTHOUGHT
It's not that horseshoeing is so hard, it's just the dread of doing it.

ON THE MAGIC TRIANGLE

I see this cohesive combination often in the setting: woman-child-horse.

It is particularly evident when a handicap is involved. It is obvious at any equine therapeutic riding center. You will see islands of woman-child-horse. Concentrate on one of those triangles, then imagine that the child on the horse...is yours.

You become hypersensitive to the slightest movement; be it protective, encouraging, or loving. Even the smallest step in this magic triangle performance going on in the arena becomes magnified. Successes are marked in the tiniest gesture, the lightest touch, the tentative smile and the skip of a heartbeat. And through the cloud that puts you in the triangle, you hear the softest of voices saying, "It's alright, he won't hurt you."

AFTERTHOUGHT

"Amigo, my friend, so true to the end.
Eras buen caballo, amigo my friend."
- Buffum and Fleming, Amigo

ON GEARS ON A HORSE

Daylight out on the trail. The riders are in a long trot. The gait of your horse would be described as 'plodding.' Every five minutes you have to catch up.

When everybody swings back to the barn, suddenly your horse becomes a muskrat in a squirrel cage! He's jiggin' and throwin' his head, chomping on the bit and whinnying like an Alpine yodeler!

You're trying to have a conversation with a new friend. After five unintelligible minutes she remarks that she used to stutter too, and offers the number of her speech therapist.

Unsaddled, you walk off the dizzyness and try to remember why you paid money for the sorry nag. You should have paid more attention because now you realize he was not given that name because of his color, Giddyup Paint Shaker!

AFTERTHOUGHT

"I believe he saw me comin'; horse traders usually do..."
from Poo Bah, by Baxter Black

44

ON BEING DELIBERATE

"If you're in a hurry, be deliberate."

It always fascinated me that Charmayne James' horse Scamper looked like he was running slower than the others, but his time was always faster. Was his stride longer? Was his body longer? Were his legs longer? Did it take less strides to go the same distance? Or was each step done with such precision that it eliminated even the slightest misstep that would add micro-seconds to the run?

I have concluded it's better to take that extra second throwing three wraps and a hooey, cutting that ear mark, driving that nail or buttoning your shirt...And do it with the same concentration that you thread a needle or put a Q-tip in your ear.

Focus, keep your eye on the ball, be deliberate. Thanks for the lesson Charmayne and Scamper.

AFTERTHOUGHT
Anlkadhtlid;s;apoliet eto tpnongljeryrypp (and this applies to typing, too.)

Rodeos

ON RODEO CLOWNS

Rodeo clowns, bullfighters and barrelmen are categorized as 'personnel' in rodeo parlance, along with secretaries, timers and announcers. That's like categorizing a kamikaze pilot with the guy that washes your windshield!

I've never known one rodeo clown who is not serious about his job.

Every time the gate swings open they walk into the tiger's cage armed with courage, quick reflexes, and experience tempered under fire. They demonstrate all the grace and guts and glory that we associate with the superhuman aspects of our cowboy game...rodeo!

AFTERTHOUGHT
John Wayne's got nothing on Wacey Munsell.

ON THE HEELER MENTALITY

"What happened to your head?" my wife asked.

"I had a little hair trim."

"You cut it yourself, didn't you?"

"It was...it was just the 'heeler mentality.'" That stopped her. The heeler mentality is where instinct often overwhelms good judgment.

And it makes life easier. Drop a sandwich, pick it up and eat it. Do a rectal exam on a cow without a plastic sleeve. Get mud on your new boots. Climb on a bad horse. Get a D in Algebra or cut your nose off to spite your face!

So cutting my own hair is not out of character, even though my barber said I looked like I used an electric sander and a weed eater.

AFTERTHOUGHT
A header has ulcers, a heeler has a hangover.

48

ON CERTIFIED BUCKLE BUNNIES

TEAM ROPERS and TRAINERS

TEAM ROPERS AND TRAINERS
...Need a dolly? Finished Girlfriend
Available: 23 years old, fine boned,
plenty of chrome, current driver's license,
CDL qualified, some shoeing experience, can
warm up the rough ones, has been hauled to
USTRC/USTR jackpots and PRCA rodeos,
low maintenance, likes Mountain Dew and
bologna, can play pitch and has no desire to
become a barrel racer.

AFTERTHOUGHT

*If you don't rope right-handed, you'll never be able
to borrow a horse. On the other hand, if you rope
left-handed no one will borrow your horse...same for
a guitar!*

ON BEING LEFT-HANDED

I'm left-handed so I am condemned to roping the heels. I play the guitar right-handed because my Dad made me. So now I can never play music or rope like the big boys.

I suffer with cacography; illegible hand writing. I autograph books upside down. I do. It's read-able.

People watch me signing my name and think it is a parlor trick. "How long did it take you to learn that?" they ask. It is like asking a one leg-ged man how long it took him to learn to limp. I'm not doing it on purpose...it's a handicap!

It's like being a bolt with Machine Threads surrounded by Nuts all drilled for Standard!

AFTERTHOUGHT
Cacography: scrambled writing.
A crumbled cross of calligraphy and cacophony.

ON BRONC YEARS

They are a measure of time like Dog Years. A Bronc Year is equivalent to 2 Roper Years. In other words, a roper should be able to compete in rodeo twice as long as a Rough Stock Rider.

When ropers show up they're pulling their three-horse slant trailer with living quarters, monster truck, a laptop, satellite dish, exercise video, a roping dummy and their jammys.

Whereas, the Rough Stock Riders arrive on Bronc Time, during the Grand Entry, with a riggin', two miles of bandage, and a dirty shirt.

So, according to Bronc Time, if our old-timer rode the rough stock till he was 56 years old, his son could still be entering Pendleton in 2046! Then he could switch to roping steers and go for another ten!

But, it all depends on whether he can find a "Woman with a Job!"

AFTERTHOUGHT
If you could kick the person in the pants responsible for most of your trouble, you wouldn't sit for a month."
- Theodore Roosevelt

ON THE MECHANICAL BULL

"So, what's the difference between riding a mechanical bull and riding the real one?" asked the boy of his dad.

"You will know the difference, my son, the first time you climb over the buckin' chute and look down."

Riding bulls is better compared to standing outside during a tornado, arm wrestling an octopus, or walking in a cage with a grizzly bear!

The bull bangs his horns on the steel chute, mashes your leg, you can feel his body heat and his feral tension. It smells like a storm is coming. You can feel your nerves running through your veins. You are totally spring-loaded, shivering, focused.

Dad says, "Nod your head when you are ready."

The son nods his head and they explode from the chute together.
- from *Lessons from a Desperado Poet* by baxter black

ON A CRUDE CARPENTARY TIP

If you ever need to split a telephone pole length-wise with a chain saw and have two flat sides, here's how:

Take a telephone pole, chalk the line, straddle it and then cut a half-inch deep slash, pulling the full length...then TURN AROUND, straddle and cut the opposite direction another half-inch deep.

They make great corrals, alleys and beams. In my dream I was cutting ice in the Arctic and split the Bering Strait lengthwise and back! The Russians said I had good straddle.

AFTERTHOUGHT
"How to deal with Ischeal Tuberosity Inflammation, better known as "noazitol."

ON JUST A MISUNDERSTANDING

Hector, a Columbian, became a citizen. One evening on the way home from a party he was pulled over for "Driving Under the Influence."

Hector walked the line, no problem. For the next test, as Hector understood it, was to...'take a blow' on the back of the officer's hand.

"How hard?" asked Hector, puzzled.

"As hard as you can," directed the law.

Hector told me he took a deep breath, reared back and hit the officer's outstretched hand so hard his handcuffs jingled!

AFTERTHOUGHT
I was charged with drunk driving and I pled "Maybe"

Farmers

ON WHY NO FARMER POETRY?

For some reason a cowboy getting bucked off is funny. It starts with the cowboy saying, "Whataya mean I can't ride that horse?" or "Don't worry, dogs really like me!"

And somehow the cowboy always ends up the butt of the joke...and that's funny!

On the other hand, farmer wrecks are always about machinery; caught in the PTO or being hit by a chemical spraying drone. So that's why I don't write more farmer poetry.

Of course, there's always the one about the farmer's daughter!

AFTERTHOUGHT
Why do they put criminals pictures in the Post Office? Why not put their pictures on postage stamps so the mailman can get a good look before he delivers the mail?

ON THE RAIN HOTLINE

When it rains at my house we all call our neighbors to compare. Usually the one who tells first, gets less!

One of the rights of farmers is to have an opinion on the weather. I try to keep abreast. I study the TV weather map with its big smiling yellow sun and the white clouds that look like giant puffs from Thomas the Tank Engine. Of course, it seems every time I watch the local forecast, the weather girl is standing in front of my state!

Oh, well, I better go check the rain gauge. I'm guessing maybe a trace, but every little bit counts.

AFTERTHOUGHT
When windmills were abundant we could tell the direction of the wind. Nowdays you have to look for a plastic grocery sack stuck in the fence! - Butch Conner

ON PAT RICHARDSON'S COLLATERALISMS

GIRL: "When we get married, I want to share all your worries, troubles and lighten your burden."

BOY: *"It's kind of you, darling, but I don't have any worries or troubles."*

GIRL: "Well, that's because we aren't married yet."

★ I looked down at the end of the bar and said to Pat, "That's us in ten years." He said, "That's a mirror."

★ Behind every great man is...a woman rolling her eyes.

★ On the journey of life, he chose the psycho-path.

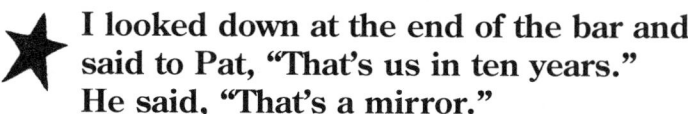

★ On his resume he said he was a bartender at the Betty Ford Clinic.

★ Ever wonder what is the speed of Dark?

ON CLAIMING TO BE A DAIRYMAN

I've never claimed to be a Dairyman and I've got the scars to prove it!

Narcolepsy, deafness, a Dutch accent and one thumb missing from the time my coverall sleeve hung up in the feeder belt dragging me across the stanchions, through electric wire, hydraulic hoses, and pieces of angle iron. The Holsteins had a mass exodus!

My sleeve finally tore off, taking my thumb as we were drug through the wall to the grain room.

I spent half a day in the hospital and when they questioned the hired milker on duty, he said he'd been listening to Led Zeppelin on his iPod and hadn't heard a thing!

AFTERTHOUGHT
"I got my tongue tangled around my eye teeth and I couldn't see what I was saying!" – Vikki's Grandpa Bill

ON TEAMWORK ON THE FARM

JB and Deb were coming back across the pasture, her walking, him riding the Polaris Ranger. "Hop up here, darlin'," he invited. She did and put her arm around his shoulders. A skunk wobbled out of the grass and onto the trail.

"Don't you be thinkin' what I know yer thinkin'." she said flatly.

"What do you mean?" he asked.

"You know what I mean . . . runnin' over him. Don't you even be thinkin' that."

"Aw," he said, "How can you think I'd do something as dumb, insane or stupid as runnin' over a skunk!"

"Ya know," she said, "That's what I told my mother when she asked if I was gonna marry YOU!"

AFTERTHOUGHT
I'm cutting back on my life insurance. I'm getting scared of my kids!

ON VIRTUAL FARMER IDOL

Contestants included:

a) A soybean farmer who sculpts tofu,
b) A sheepman who knits wool into the shape of a coyote, And...
c) A chicken farmer who puts Tabasco sauce in his pullet feed to stimulate 'hot wings!'

But the winner was an Illinois fish farmer who invented the Asian Carpcake, Carp-legs, the Carp-apple tree, even carpgrass for your lawn! His theme song was, "I've got the Carp, You've got the Carp, Everybody's got the Carp!"

It was actually his second time. He had tried the year before when he was a crab fisherman in Maryland. He was disqualified when the judges heard his theme song!

AFTERTHOUGHT
His astrologer said his sign was FECES.

ON THE PRESIDENT'S WIFE'S GARDEN

She has taken an interest in gardening. She recommends Organic, which is fashionable. I support her efforts. I have a garden, too.

But between her and me, we could hardly feed ourselves for a week, much less our neighbors.

So, we lay that responsibility on the shoulders of our country's farmers and ranchers, who, by using modern agricultural practices ensure that our children will not go to bed hungry tonight.

AFTERTHOUGHT

The world owes our prosperity, in great part, to people who work for companies like Dow, Monsanto, Pfizer, Pioneer, Case, Elanco and the A&M colleges from sea to shining sea. Say thanks to them when you sit down at supper tonight. They are our Horn of Plenty.

ON DISPOSABLE TAILGATES

My Iowa friend Steve has a history of minor collisions.

Turns out he had unhooked the gooseneck, forgot to drop the tailgate and drove off. Next day, tailgate down, he jumped in the cab, glanced in the rear view and backed into the meter pole. He swore someone had moved it while he was in the shop!

Last month we pulled out of his circle drive-way and he hit a low flatbed trailer. I heard a screech, felt a bump and could hear something dragging in the gravel, however, it didn't seem to slow the truck any.

"I think you hit something," I said, "Should we stop and check?"

"Whatever," he said, and drove on.

AFTERTHOUGHT
A car will last a lifetime if you're careless enough.

ON FOWL PLAY

It was a hot summer morning when Darrie's dog Billie, got into the neighbor's chicken yard and created havoc. She was distraught and offered to pay restitution.

"Well, they're not dead," said the neighbor, "Your dog didn't kill them, she just plucked 'em all!"

"What can I do?" asked the contrite Darrie.

"Well, I am worried about them getting heat stroke."

"Oh, okay," Darrie said, "I'll run home and get some sunscreen."

"Either that," said the neighbor, "Or barbecue sauce!"

AFTERTHOUGHT
If life gives you llamas . . . make llamanade.

ON A HAPPY DAY IN THE MILKING BARN

When someone tells me they grew up on a dairy farm I say, "You have paid your dues, my son."

'Cause, let's face it, milkin' 12 head of cows by hand in a bucket before breakfast every morning is hard labor AND there's a few ol' timers that can remember doing it! You can find them in nursing homes after retiring from a comfortable life of working for Merck, DeLaval, Progressive Dairyman or Ohio Farm and Dairy. They ran away from home!

AFTERTHOUGHT

Dr. Eng commented that dairy cattle are not very popular with the cowboys in the feedyard. He said, "It's hard to be a cowboy when the steers are following you around!"

ON BONELESS CHICKEN

KFC is planning to market "boneless chicken!" I'm not surprised, who needs wings? The next step could be invertebrate Chicken. It could have an exoskeleton like lobsters and big beetles.

Or they could be planted like oysters in a shell or barnacles on a pier. How 'bout chicken meat in a 5 pound egg? Basically an egg with a head. "Easy to feed, easy to gather, easy to entertain!" The possibilities are endless! Spooky.

It's been a long time since I've had chicken like Aunt Effie used to make. She used Crisco. It had a flavor of its own. Now it seems that chicken tastes like whatever you put on it. It's like feathered tofu. Oh, well.

AFTERTHOUGHT
Good luck to KFC. As I've always said, I eat all the eggs I can. It's one less chicken I have to contend with!

ON GOOD TIMES UP NORTH

I was in the Ag Expo building. The temperature outside was 3 degrees. I stopped at a booth of a man selling wood stoves.

"How things going?" I asked. "Well," he said, "You know how things are."

I DID know how things were. He was in the midst of prosperity! North Dakota was booming!

I tried to find something positive for him to say like..."The doctor said I was only twenty pounds overweight," or "The pipes didn't freeze."

But I said instead, "Accounting for the recession, I'd say you're doin' pretty good."

"Yeah," he said, "But I have to live here."

"Well, just hang on," I said, "And pray for global warming!"

AFTERTHOUGHT
Life is like a septic tank, you get out of it what you put in.

Vets

and
Dogs

ON THE PRESENCE OF NOTHING

A vet student was palpating a cow for pregnancy. She withdrew her hand and said, "I couldn't feel anything. Maybe she's open?"

Not feeling anything, is not a diagnosis.

CONCEPT #1 You must grasp that "Open" is not the absence of something; it is the presence of nothing.

To wit; people might think that a hole is something. But a hole is nothing. A hole does not exist. So if you are looking for a hole, you are looking for nothing.

When palpating, to call a cow Open one must find the presence of nothing by a thorough search. Then if you find nothing, something is not there.

AFTERTHOUGHT
CONCEPT #2 Regardless of your professional opinion, a female of the species "MIGHT" be pregnant but she is never 'ALMOST' pregnant."

ON THE VETERINARIAN'S HUSBAND

He approaches the refrigerator with trepidation since that evening he thawed out a piece of steak and fried it for himself. She was out on call.

Next morning she was hunting through the freezer for a sample she had labeled, "possible tissue damage from Hypoderma lineatum" to send to the lab.

"Honey," she said, "Did you see a..." then glimpsed in the trash can and saw her writing on a big plastic baggie.

"What?" he asked.

"Oh, nothing," she said, "I'm pretty sure it was a necrotizing cattle grub anyway."

AFTERTHOUGHT
The cobbler's children have no shoe polish.

ON "ET TU, UTERI!"

"We've got a prolapse and need you to come to the ranch straight away," the lady rancher said.

"I've got this clinic here, eh?" he offered. "Nay," she said, "it's too far, she's too big and she's down!"

An hour later Doc was looking at the big cow, with a prolapse that looked like a four-foot long breakfast burrito. With the rancher's help they tied the cow to her Polaris...then the wreck began! Use your imagination; chaos, havoc, anarchy, cataclysm, and messy mutual destruction.

The cow finally tangled in the line and attacked the good doctor whilst converting the 4-wheeler into a 3-wheeler!

The unlady-like rancher was screaming, "Why does this always happen to me?!"

"I've got this clinic now, eh?" said Dr. Blaine.

AFTERTHOUGHT
"Et tu uteri!" Snakespeare (1598)

ON TALKIN' TO THE DOG

I said, "Okie, what are ya thinkin'?"
"School," he said, "Maybe goin' to college."

"What would you major in?"
"Bones, I guess."

"An anatomy student?"
"No, a chef. Specialize in bones, like Colonel Sanders does with chicken."

"Sounds interesting, but where are you going to get a regular source of bones?"
"I've got a cousin in Miles City named Badgett. He said them bones were just like sheep up there, covered the country."

I looked at Okie. I knew he'd never make it to Montana. But I thought to myself, it's nice to know that even good ol' farm dogs dream big. Kinda like good ol' farmers.

AFTERTHOUGHT
If horses have nightmares do dogs have night bit....?
Oops.

ON THOUGHTS OF THE VETERINARY PROFESSION:

Why a barber and a surgeon should never say, "Oops!"

The plethora of chicken/the dearth of poultry practitioners.

Is there a place for grooming in an exclusive reptile practice?

What do you think of men in veterinary practice? A thing of the past?

The future of leather shoes, purses and seat covers made of dog hide.

Body piercing in vet med; fashion statement or cruelty?

The use of a wood chipper in poultry euthanasia?

AFTERTHOUGHT
What do you tell the parents of a child who wants to go to vet school?

73

ON THE FREEDOM OF INFERTILITY

The heifer Dr. Darrell was palpating had no uterus and no ovaries! "This heifer is open," he told Mario the client, "She's a freemartin."

Mario looked puzzled. The good doctor explained the congenital condition, defined hermaphrodite, and that she would never be fertile.

Mario nodded seriously, then turned her out of the chute. He instructed his helper, "Put her back in with the bulls, her ovaries haven't come down yet!"

AFTERTHOUGHT
When freemartin really means free.

ON PREGNANCY CHECKING THE EASY WAY

I went down to inventory a herd of cows the company was buying. With the crew I preg-tested 2,200 head and sorted them into Open, Bred and Old. It took three days.

To finalize the deal the boss sent down a crusty ol' cattle buyer named Harold.

I woke up next morning to find Harold had turned the cows all back together and was gate cutting them himself in the long alley! I was stunned, mad and bumfuzzled!

"Sorry you wasted your time, Sonny," he said, "Anybody can tell if they are old. And I can tell if they're bred by the way the hair lays on their back!"

AFTERTHOUGHT

Modern veterinary medicine can now use ultrasound and blood tests to determine pregnancy. But they've got nothing on Harold. He could tell without getting his hands dirty!

ON GIMP

Charlie has a cowdog named Gimp. He has established a breeding program and now has produced a litter of pups that all limp. His theory is that it will save an enormous amount of time, getting a cowdog to the bum leg-ged stage.

And...he stressed, it is humane since they won't have to go through the agony of getting injured in the first place!

It might be a good idea, but Charlie, like me, is gettin' a little long in the tooth. We're thinkin' like old dogs. Young dogs think work is play. They turn over a new rock everyday. Fun to watch.

AFTERTHOUGHT

Ah, it just makes me feel like a puppy again.

ON THE POWER OF
INHERITED JUDGMENT

Doc went out to an 800-head Nevada cow ranch that had never done preg-checking and culling...ol' Grandpa didn't believe in it.

But the young Grandchild rancher wanted to modernize. Doc sorted cattle into Open or Bred and found a 50% conception rate.

All done, Doc glanced up to see the young rancher mixing the cows back together! The Grandchild rancher acknowledged it was good to know how many calves to expect, but Grandpa always said the place would run 800 cows...and who could argue with that?

AFTERTHOUGHT
It's mathematical and perfectly subintractable.

ON RUDY

Rudy, my new dog, has been a boisterous, happy, destructive puppy. At 6 months he is a universal shredder! This week he has chewed through my good heavy-duty fifty-foot rubber hose.

I gave him the "Bad Dog!" and spanked him with the hose. To test him I left the chewed hose in plain sight overnight. Next morning I found it on the other side of the corral.

I called him. He slunk up to me cowering and said, "I didn't mean to do it! I forgot! It was just sittin' there! I was cleaning up the yard! The barn cat made me do it! The coyotes moved it! Blame it on the NRA, PBR, FFA, NBA, CIO..." then he paused and said, "What difference does it make anyway?"

AFTERTHOUGHT
Looks like I'm gonna have to restrict his cable TV habits.

78

ON CLAIMING TO BE A SMALL ANIMAL VET

I never claimed to be a small animal vet and I've got the scars to prove it!

Not a decent tie to my name, at least 50 mongrel dogs named for me, and twenty parallel scars up and down my left arm while trying to pluck a grass awn from the ear of an unbroken barn cat.

I had gotten him in a towel. I desperately clung to his scruff as he mauled my arm like I'd been picking blackberries in a bob wire patch!

The awn fell out by itself. I no longer make house calls and, on the bright side, the scars obliterated the tattoo of my ex-fiancee's name who eventually married the dentist.

AFTERTHOUGHT

If you don't take off the tourniquet you'll get gangrene. If you take it off you'll bleed to death. It's a choice.

79

ON VETERINARIAL INJURIES

For probably the jillionth time I reached my right hand into the horse's mouth, grasped the tongue, pulled it out of the left side of his mouth and peeked in.

I was looking at his upper and lower right molars for signs of "proper" wear. The best description of the chewing mechanism is "... a pair of scissors 2 foot long, razor sharp, scalloped blades that can close with 800 lbs of pressure."

And, of course, I put my bare left arm into his mouth and felt the incisive edges of the molars, with my fingers, both upper and lower to detect the jagged ridges that can cut the oral mucosa, or a finger, I guess.

AFTERTHOUGHT
Just another day in the profession that is ranked as #2 in "most dangerous jobs." Airline pilots ranked #1 above 'animal care and service worker.'

Workin' Cattle

ON THE MUD BATH

Kadie is a Montana rancher who enjoys her feminine side. She had clipped out an ad for a spa that included a hot tub, massage, pedicure and mud bath. The morning of the appointment she was doing the pre-dawn heifer check.

Right off she found a muddy newborn in trouble. She loaded the wet, slimy calf onto the sled and started back to the barn. Kadie only went down, once soaking her entire left side.

Then leaning into the sled rope she fell flat on her face! She looked like a chocolate eclaire.

Twenty minutes later she hobbled into the bathroom and looked in the mirror. Then the list caught her eye. "I guess," she said to nobody in particular, "I can cross out the mud bath."

AFTERTHOUGHT
"Say, Babe, nobody can light a candle under you!"

ON WORKING MOTHERS

Pam and I were discussing cow psychology, like when mama cows go to water, who decides which one will stay behind and babysit?

We've never seen them drawing straws or guessing the number of dewclaws behind their back. Pam said since they have no written language they didn't take turns. But I imagined it must have something to do with the pecking order?

She agreed it's Nature's Way of separating the argumentative from the thirsty.

I asked her what she meant? "You wouldn't understand," she said.

I asked if this had anything to do with working mothers?

"Don't even go there," she said.

AFTERTHOUGHT
I've watched mothers feed their babies with tiny little spoons and forks. I wonder what Chinese mothers use? Toothpicks?

ON ANOTHER SQUEEZE CHUTE STORY

I went to help my neighbor work cows; shots, preg test, brand and pour on. I gasped at his squeeze chute!

There was a cow's head pokin' through the tailgate, then on her side, then on her knees, then with a foot stickin' out!

Monty said working the head gate was like trying to fight an octopus! Whitey clung to the thrashing cow's head trying to check her teeth!

We worked 106 cows in two hours, missed catching 12 head, set three on fire and had to guess the age of the last five. Just another romantic cowboy day.

EPILOGUE

Six days later the squeeze chute was euthanized and is now a cattle guard on a dirt road somewhere to nowhere in the great southwest. May it Rest In Pieces.

ON THE FATHER OF THE BRIDE

Kurt borrowed the neighbor's surrey for his daughter's wedding and immediately wrecked it! His face looked like somebody scraped it with a cheese grater!

They were 80 miles from a hospital and 4 hours to the wedding so Jolene, the bridesmaid, and a nurse offered to "Sew him up!"

After the triage was completed, the only bandage she could find was a Pampers one of the mothers lent him.

As for the wedding, the bride rode in on a hay wagon and every wedding photo in the scrapbook showed dear ol' Dad doin' his part, in right-side profile.

I don't know if it was his smile or the Pampers, but from that day on he was called "Baby Face!"

AFTERTHOUGHT

Have you ever noticed that the father of the groom is irrelevant.

ON THE SCARS TO PROVE IT

I never claimed to be a cowman and I've got the scars to prove it!

Frostbit fingers, baler twine blisters, and an odd scrape on the side of my head where the hair won't grow back from when my good ol' horse slipped down on an ice slick in the calving lot.

I went out off the front quarter, hung my left spur on the canvas medicine bag that was looped over the horn with parachute cord and lost a chunk of my ear when he drug me, unconscious, over the rusty metal feeder by the gate.

It, my ear, now looks like a ball of string!

AFTERTHOUGHT
It interferes with my hearing but I get half-off at the ear bud store.

ON THE COMPASSIONATE COWMAN

Willie's wife always praised his bovine obstetrical touch. "You're really good at that, Honey," she said, as he headed out to the calving barn.

Ten minutes later he found himself flat on his back, with one boot missing, his jeans down around his ankles, his white legs sandpapered, scratched and scraped, but thankfully, he still had the ability to move his wrist.

He limped into the house aching for some comfort, maybe praise. His darlin' wife looked at him and said, "You're lucky to be alive!"

Willie conjured on that, then asked, "If I was dead, would you come and look for me?"

"Of course," she said, "When Desperate Housewives was over."

AFTERTHOUGHT
If you can't be kind, at least have the decency to be vague.

IN THE BLOOD

An ol' timer came to help preg test the cows last fall. He stood on the catwalk and helped push 'em in. I asked him if he didn't get tired of doin' this. He said, "Son, when workin' cows becomes a chore, I guess I'll know I'm done."

AFTERTHOUGHT

You can't just quit a cow, sometimes you're all she's got...
No reinforcements in the hall, no 9-1-1 to hear her call, just you...
Nobody else, that's all, to get her through the spot.

- From Working for Wages, baxter black

C🐂w
Bidness

ON ROMANTIC QUOTES FROM "HEY, COWGIRL NEED A RIDE?"

"The pilot light in Lick's heart flared briefly. Not a ventricle stopper, but the interest was there. The furnace didn't kick on, but it was put on notice."

"She'd always been innately aware of her own seductiveness and its effect on mortal men."

"She broached the subject indirectly, setting a trap as neatly as a tunnel spider spins her web."

"Her diaphanous dress clung to her curves like a wet tee shirt on the Statue of Liberty."

"Being with her was like driving a Maserati for the first time, like seeing Halley's comet, or discovering that the chocolate really did go all the way to the bottom of the cone in a Drumstick."

"What do you care about?" he asked, like a mastodon sliding into La Brea.

"I told you. I want to marry you," he stated. She didn't say, "I'd rather go to jail, go down with the Titanic, or move to Wendover." He was encouraged.

"Why, glory be. You're alive! You were just playing posthumously!" said the old man, mangling his marsupials.

ON THE OBVIOUS

"The data is clear – Calves that arrive healthy and stay healthy at the feedlot make more money."

This was printed in bold letters at the beginning of the article. I read it again. What's the catch? Am I missing something? Do calves who stay healthy, etc, have better eyesight, higher IQ, a greater chance of being featured in a vaccine ad?

Apparently what is obvious to some of us isn't always obvious to everyone. Can you imagine this question in a college Animal Science quiz: *Do cattle that arrive healthy in the feedlot make more money than those who arrive sick and stay sick? True or false?* This could be good for a Master's thesis!

AFTERTHOUGHT

But sometimes the logic becomes crystal clear. I overheard a cattle feeder remark, "The calves that got sick and died right away, made more that those that lingered on and died eventually."

ON WHO MAKES A LIVIN'
IN THE COW BIDNESS

 The dairyman who works harder than an Egyptian hod carrier and lives between buy outs.

 A packing house buyer who spends his day drawing blood from cattle feeders and is learning to speak Portuguese.

The economist who is a master at economic monetary capability, which is just what it sounds.

 The cattle feeder who keeps rewinding THE ALAMO movie thinking "Surely Davy Crockett's bound to win sooner or later!"

 The stocker-grower who haunts sale barns gambling on each bid. You've got to admire someone who brags he only has a 10% death loss.

And the lonely cow-calf operator where lifestyle is counted as a financial asset.

AFTERTHOUGHT

As for me I try to align myself with the PGA, the NBA and the NRA, "Shoot for the center!"

ON A WORLD WITHOUT COWS

My first observation would be, there would be no Big Macs, beef, milk or cheese. We'd hear, "Pork, it's what's for dinner! Where's the Tofu? Goat, the other white meat, Got Okra? Certified Angus Drumstick?"

We'd be importing insulin made from Yak pancreas. Roy Rogers would have stayed in Iowa and become the Soybean Balladeer.

Trevor Brazile would become a professional golfer and I would be a former reptile veterinarian and Swineherd Poet!

"Ode to the Pig,
Who brings us ribs and pork
Oh, how I long to trade my Ham
for Sirloin on a Fork!"

AFTERTHOUGHT
"I'll have some cold mutton gravy with hair in it."

ON SUSPICIOUS OF THE GOOD COW MARKET

I was braggin' to Bill that I had sold 520 lb feeder cattle for $2.50 a pound!

"I know," he said, "I've sold some myself but..." then he paused, "I wonder if the price is getting too high?"

I cast a skeptical eye, but he was serious. "Whataya mean?" I asked.

"Is it possible that the price will drive people away from beef and ruin our business?"

I immediately thought of that Yogi Berra observation, "The place is so crowded, nobody goes there!"

AFTERTHOUGHT
They say a watched pot never boils. I say a boiled watch won't keep time.

ON ONLINE DATING RURALMATE.NET

ATTENTION! ITINERATE MUSICIAN AND / OR TRUCK DRIVER:

Perfect girlfriend for itinerate musician and/or truck driver...Young, open but has some pasture exposure, loves your music, is tone deaf, her favorite meal is breakfast at Waffle House at 1:00am, can drive (her brother was a moonshiner), can change a tire, go for three days without sleep on nothing but Skoal and Monster drinks. Some would say she has a very friendly nature, everybody in the band, anyway, and she will meet up with you anywhere between Nashville and Williston, ND. *Warning:* She has been known to prance on occasion.

AFTERTHOUGHT

They say a stitch in time saves nine, but will it keep a mime in stitches?

ON IT'S WOMAN'S WORK

How many times have you heard some rancher or farmer introduce his wife as, "This is my wife, she does the books."

I do it myself! I can't tell you what my electric bill is, how much money we have in the bank, who insures the shop, who we still owe money to, or if our kids are coming home for Thanksgiving, but she can. So I don't have to worry.

I have more important things to do; shoe the horse, fix the water line, get the tank heaters ready for winter, catch Cattlemen to Cattlemen on RFD-TV (I consider it continuing education) and find a 5/16 nut for the float arm. I'm on the job doin' Man's Work!

I remember being so busy one time that I asked my wife if we could afford a hired man. She said, "What are you talkin' about? I've already got a good one!"

AFTERTHOUGHT
If you order a BLT you get tomato. If you order a BLT without tomato, you don't get a BLT.

ON COWBOY ADVICE TO THE LOVELORN NO.2

Dear Mr. Cowboy,
My husband has come into some inheritance. We need food for the twins and a refrigerator that works but he wants to invest it in a four-wheeler to pull his roping dummy at the funeral in honor of his dead uncle. Am I being selfish?

Signed, Timorous In Tulare

DEAR TIMEROUS,
Make sure he gets one with four-wheel drive and the beer cooler attachment.

Dear Mr. Cowboy,
I'm courting a shiny lookin' dolly who wants to get married but she's been engaged to half the men in Modesto. Should that concern me?

Signed, Reluctant Rouser

DEAR RELUCK,
Shiny is always good. Besides, Modesto ain't that big.

ON BEETLESS TUESDAY

The social engineers have been trying to force Meatless Monday on children. The reason, pick one: "Save the Whales! Improve gas mileage? Lose weight? Global Warming? Build a Wall to keep out riff-raff?"

If they really want to make a difference, let's look at some other options.

How 'bout BEETLESS TUESDAY! It's a three-purpose vegetable; A Tuber of Play, A Tuber of Art and a Tuber Time Piece . . . sound silly?

Let's get serious...NO POWER WEDNESDAY? COFFEELESS THURSDAY! A YEAR WITH-OUT LATTES! BEN & JERRY'S SUNDAY-LESS SUNDAE!

Well, it is easy to ridicule our fellow Americans who build their little fiefdoms with good intent. Be real . . . I'm suggesting TAXLESS TUESDAY! Everything you earn on Tuesdays you get to keep!

Which makes more sense to you...
$1,362 or not eating BEETS ON TUESDAY?

AFTERTHOUGHT
Maybe it's just me.

ON THE FUTURE OF COWS

Studies have shown that the difference between the top third of a pen of steers and the bottom third can be as high as 40%!

It makes sense to selectively breed for these more efficient, productive cattle. Genetics will be the key.

In fifty years, questions of 'man-made' Global Warming may be proven or forgotten like the Global Cooling, Worldwide Famine or Y2K collapse.

Regardless, agricultural research, private and public will be at the forefront. Agriculture can't put a man on the moon, but we can feed China.

AFTERTHOUGHT
This is all well and good, but when will we breed cattle that can be potty trained?

ON PAT RICHARDSON'S AGRIGATIONS

I was thinking about how people read the Bible more as they get older; then it dawned on me...they're cramming for their final exam.

I like those exercise programs on TV. I used to watch golf but my doctor said I wasn't getting enough exercise, so now I watch tennis.

He has so many bill collectors behind him, they have to car pool.

If we're here to help others, then what exactly are others here for?

Developers bulldoze out the trees then name the streets after them.

I took an IQ test.
The results were negative.

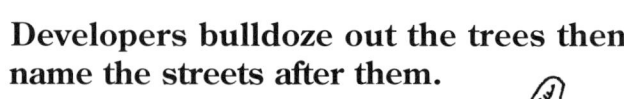

ON RULES OF BEHAVIOR IN SPOONING

Ah, men discussing women. It's like cavemen discussing the internal combustion engine.

Men are grounded in the barter technique. They understand flowers for a kiss, candlelight for a hug, fraternity ring for a peek, and engagement ring for what's behind Door Number One.

The rules governing men's behavior are as simple as the card game War...high card wins.

The rules women play by cover reams of single-spaced, small-font computer printouts in which exceptions abide, words are made up, as in "change on your dresser" is called "loose change," and clarification of "what she really means" is as comprehensible as Mongolian throat singing.

- from novel *Ride, Cowboy, Ride!* by baxter black

AFTERTHOUGHT
"We have one thing on our side," he said, "They need us to continue the species."

"Not for long, brother. They're cloning sheep now!"

Seriously,

ELECTORAL
COLLEGE
GRADUATE

Sort Of

ON THE CRYPT ORCHID IS KING

"In the land of geldings, the crypt orchid is king."

Government bureaucracy is the pre-eminent example of Peter's Principle. We are governed by the lowest common denominator.

I don't know which is more unintelligibly obtuse; a politician being interviewed by a reporter OR an NFL offensive pass receiver being questioned about his performance.

Lack of character did not begin with Nixon or end with Clinton. The most we can expect from our leaders is "not to make it worse."

AFTERTHOUGHT

On a lighter note try this: while watching them squawk politico-media blather on television with their talk show accomplices, turn the sound down. Then imagine they are actors on a reality show discussing hemorrhoid medications. At least it would be more believable.

ON THE VIRUS, FORMALLY KNOWN AS SWINE FLU

When the Asian Flu hit the country were people warned to stay away from Chinese restaurants? When West Nile virus was diagnosed did they tell us to avoid going to Egypt? How 'bout small pox? Were there Dwarf Warnings posted? Do you catch the Swine Flu by eating BBQ spare ribs?

NO! So why did the demand for pork in supermarkets and restaurants plummet? The public had no clue. They were, "playing it safe."

But they had no more chance of catching swine flu from eating pork, than getting a tattoo on their back saying KICK ME!

AFTERTHOUGHT
Rumors ride in the Diamond Lane and facts putter along behind.

ON SUSTAINABLE FARMING? REALLY?

New Age gurus are proposing a return to farming methods used in the first half of the 20th century. They refer to it as "Sustainable Farming."

After WWII the world's population exploded! 1970 scientists were convinced a new Ice Age was coming and Global Starvation was imminent! But help was on the way!

Monsanto, Dow, John Deere, Pfizer, Monfort, Pioneer, plus a battalion of academic and privately funded scientists were knee deep in research to feed the increasing masses. And look around you friends. They did it...and saved the world.

Using modern agricultural science we can feed ourselves and our neighbors. That is the definition of SUSTAINABLE FARMING!

For the sake of clarity, a more accurate definition of someone who is lucky if they can feed themselves, much less their neighbor, would be called SUBSISTENCE LEVEL FARMING.

AFTERTHOUGHT

subsistence: syn. (Poverty, Insufficient, Hand to Mouth) Roget's Thesaurus

ON FOOD, CLOTHING AND SHELTER

The latest eco-news/slant de jour is the hysteric 'discovery' that cows release more methane than all the cars in the country! It's true. It's also true that cows produce more milk than all the cars in the U.S.! Yes, it's true!

Methane is one of the three Greenhouse gasses along with Nitrous Oxide and Carbon Dioxide (CO2). Methane is created by fermentation like city landfills, rice growing, dairy cows, wetlands and composting. It comprises 16% of the Greenhouse gasses.

Carbon dioxide sources are primarily fossil fuels, their recovery and use. CO2 comprises 76% of Greenhouse gasses, with 33% of that total being created by transportation (cars and trucks).

So, conceding that in the U.S. 30 million cows emit more methane than cars...and that 125 million cars produce more total Greenhouse gasses than cows, which is worse for our environment? Hard to say which is more essential; agriculture or transportation.

AFTERTHOUGHT
How long can you live without driving?

ON STUPID IS AS STUPID DOES

In the movie Forrest Gump, the hero was a nice man with a low IQ. When people called him stupid, his mother said, "Stupid is as stupid does."

I never quite understood what that meant?

As I have watched the ravages the Endangered Species Act has done and is doing to our land and local economies, it is obvious that the politically appointed bureaucrats have never set foot on the public and private lands or know the history of the community they destroy. They are educated and smart but ignorant.

Forrest Gump's mom is right, "You don't have to be stupid to be stupid."

AFTERTHOUGHT

Panda.org estimates up to 10,000 species go extinct every year. Name one.

ON THE TOAST

You mare ridin', mouth breathin',
egg suckin' skunk
You're the kind who drowns kittens for fun
You hat stealin', hole peepin',
pencil-necked punk
You're the blister on everyone's bun

You scrofulous wool slippin', miscreant scum
Yer the grease off a Hell's Angels' comb
You bilgewater, bog drinkin', boot lickin' bum
Yer a bucket of thundermug foam.

To sum up your good points
could be quite a chore
There's so many that it's hard to say
You're either au jus off a dog kennel floor
Or a nit in a wino's toupee

Regardless, we love ya. I don't like to boast
But our standards are really quite high
And although you seem lacking,
I'll offer a toast
'Cause the truth is, yer our kinda guy!

AFTERTHOUGHT
*Useful for dinner to offer up to your boss who has been a
jerk for 20 long years.*

ON SMOKE IN THE AIR

It's only been in the last 200 years of our continent's existence that forest fires have become an inconvenience to humans. It is a bit pretentious to think that Man, over the millennia can have much effect even though fervid bell ringers play on.

If we disappeared like dinosaurs, in a short 1,000 years the Earth would wipe out our footprints.

So, remember when you see Texas AT&T stadium or Hoover Dam or a brand new saddle, each are waiting to eventually be turned into dust.

The Earth is simply renewing itself, as it has since Genesis. Just ask Noah.

AFTERTHOUGHT

I appreciate zealots, shucksters and shysters, they can be entertaining. But they can create havoc in their wake, and you can bet they won't lift a finger or spend a pence to help you clean it up.

ON RECYCLING ISN'T PRETTY

The abhorrence of recycling is so strong that some people will object even though they know it is bettering the earth and the environment. Pink Slime is a perfect example. They destroyed a recycling process that had no down side just because the image in their brain was offensive.

I admit it would be nice to recycle old quarterbacks, cowboys and retired Army sergeants but I wonder about recycling old politicians?

I'm just not sure what you could reuse them for, although, I do have a field that needs fertilizing. I know it sounds awful but as I have noted, recycling is not pretty.

AFTERTHOUGHT
If 4 out of 5 people suffer from diarrhea . . . does that mean one out of five enjoy it?

ON THE LUDDITES

A British study shows that animals and crops raised under strict "organic" rules have no nutritional or health benefits over animals and crops grown with FDA/USDA approved insecticides, paracitacides, antibiotics, chemical disinfectants and/or growth stimulants.

As for the benefits of "Alternative Medicine," read their label:

THIS PRODUCT HAS NOT BEEN EVALUATED BY THE FOOD & DRUG ADMINISTRATION. IT IS NOT INTENDED TO DIAGNOSE, TREAT, CURE OR PREVENT ANY DISEASE.

The sales success of "natural food and magic potions" depends on the public being uninformed. The less you know, the easier the decisions. With knowledge comes responsibility, and that's the rub.

AFTERTHOUGHT
Whole Foods vs the Dollar Store...The Haves vs Have Nots

ON BIOMASS RECYCLING

For 20 years, coal-burning plants have been experimenting with Biomass as fuel. In most cases it is wood byproducts of lumber mills.

But, I'm thinking if southern power plants really want to recycle biomass, how 'bout kudzu! My gosh, it's hangin' on every power pole from Macon to Memphis! They could compost it, ensile it, or lay it out on Interstates 10 and 20 to be dried and flattened. Then cut it in chunks like peat and burn it along with the loblolly stumps and chitlins.

Why do these perfect solutions come to me so easily? I should have been a genius!

AFTERTHOUGHT
Genius? In college your blood alcohol was higher than your GPA.

112

ON SWINE RECYCLING

During the Swine Flu when the pigs were being exterminated, Egypt quickly realized that swine were a major factor in their garbage disposal industry!

But who knew? They practiced a wonderful example of recycling; People eat pigs...Pigs eat garbage...People eat pigs!

Fermenting landfills are one of the biggest emitters of methane. Why not fence the area with hog wire and reintroduce pigs? Then market them as All Natural, Free Range, Garbage-Raised Pork!

Then again, some might suspect that it's just another Pyramid scheme.
(sorry, punsters)

AFTERTHOUGHT

If your throat is sore you get hoarse. But if a pig loses his voice, he gets disgruntled. (I can't help it)

ON THE SHEEP CAMP

The Dept. of Labor is making it more difficult to hire "foreign shepherds." This is to assure they won't deprive any of the millions of unemployed able-bodied Americans, of a job.

Where does the Secretary of Labor live...in Siberia?

My question is, what able-bodied, food-stamped, receiving government checks American standing in the unemployment line today, is going to apply for an outdoor job on Blizzard Mountain, Idaho where you are on call 24 hrs a day and castrate lambs with his (or her) teeth?

Besides, any American that would make a good sheepherder is already at work in the gas fields, Iraqi pipelines and Afghanistan security patrols. As you can see, it takes a no-frill kind of person.

AFTERTHOUGHT
A quote from Congress' Minority Whip, "86% of the public thinks we're not worth a warm bucket of spit." What! Only 86%?!

ON LIFE'S LESSONS FROM
DESPERADO POET BY BAXTER BLACK

You will be amazed at how capable people think you are if they don't know you well. Don't waste that advantage.

The Chaos Theory explains why a poor checker player can never beat a good checker player but a poor chess player can beat a good chess player once.

Honesty is the best policy, life is less stressful if you aren't having to look over your shoulder at the people who are sorting through your droppings.

It's hard to be what you aren't. If you can be true to yourself and true to others at the same time, you sleep better.

There are people who live where they have to live to do what they want to do, and there are people who do what they have to do to live where they want to live.

One of the secrets of life is knowing how to take a fall; physical, financial or emotional. My usual reaction is to roll till I can see daylight.

AFTERTHOUGHT
If you can't be informative at least be entertaining.

ON BUSINESS LESSONS FROM
DESPERADO POET BY BAXTER BLACK

When it takes more that 10 minutes to explain what you do for a living, you're Self-Unemployed.

If you expect people to buy from you, make yourself easy to find.

If you want to be a writer, you need to have something to write about.

Diversity is like fishing with two rods; you've always got bait in the water

I'd rather have an honest man's handshake than a crooked man's signature.

One of life's business dictums; somebody has to put up the money or nothing happens.

CEO vs CPA. It's a Love-Hate relationship not unlike cowboys vs cows, reporters vs politicians, or lawyers vs criminals.

It's not about how much you made, it's whether they got their money's worth.

AFTERTHOUGHT
First, trust your intuitions.

Mumbles

ON DUMB BUT USEFUL

The pastor was making a point Sunday morning. He said, "Even God's dumbest creatures can be useful."

Obviously, He gave us sheep. If you were forced to live on a deserted island with only one species of animal, which would you pick?

Fish? A horse? A pack of dogs? A litter of kittens? Cows? Pigs? Alligators, Possum, Goats, Parrots?

Cows are equal to sheep in IQ and their SAT scores, but they are bulky and hard to handle. You can make a case for chickens but they would be boring company.

So, that leaves sheep as the world's best all-natural, edible, cuddly, wearable, rideable, milkable, recylable species on Earth.

AFTERTHOUGHT
Right before Astroturf, a close second.

EUSKAL HERRIA

ON THE MASTER OF NONE

It helps to know a little about a lot of things. It also allows you to make a fool of yourself in many areas.

I worked at a Parasitology lab during college. I can tell you the life cycle of Stephanofilaria tylisi.

I can tell you about the skeletal, dental, reproductive, feet and alimentary tract of the hippo, rhino, elephant, giraffe and blue whale.

I can tune a banjo, carve leather, explain apical dominance, whistle loud, age a horse by his teeth, say both red and black headed buzzards in Spanish, count to ten in Basque, write upside down and backwards, castrate a goat and kill a rattler with a rope.

AFTERTHOUGHT
What did he get on his IQ test? "Drool."

119

ON THE ART OF DRIVING DAUGHTER

Most farm kids learn to drive early on. When my daughter was 13 we were having a BBQ at our house. Uncle Andy had parked his big 3/4 ton GMC 4x4 pickup in front of the porch. We needed to move it. I asked him if Jennifer could do it.

"Sure," said Andy "The keys are in it."

She raced to the big rig and climbed in. I saw her examining the gauges and knobs. Abruptly she jumped out and came running over, "I can't drive it, Dad," she said, "I can't find the clutch!"

AFTERTHOUGHT

She was mad because she got an "F" on her driver's license.

ON HUNTING THE WILEY HOG

"There's a big one!" said Newt.

We spotted a large black creature. I asked if that was a cow...or a pig, or a small buffalo. I calculated 400 yards. "How much should I elevate the shot?" I asked.

"About this much," he instructed. I looked back to see Bwana holding his thumb and index finger about two inches apart. Does that mean two inches above the pig or two inches above the cross hairs? I hesitated. I looked back... too late...the pig was gone. My heroic moment squandered.

They cut me no slack..."This would have been a Boone and Crockett Record! They'd never seen one that big; hoof-prints like a Rhino, tusks as long as a Mastodon, enough meat to make two and a half tons of sausage!"

I felt my future melt away. Oh, well, at least we got it all on film.

AFTERTHOUGHT
How does this sound, "We shall serve no swine before its time."

121

IF IT WAS UP TO ME

I realize that if the world were up to me, it would be populated with people who had my natural limitations. We'd never have put a man on the moon, discovered the ballpoint pen, or eaten Italian food. We'd have no wheel, no fluorescent lighting or cell phone. We'd never have discovered Greenland or Antarctica, Cream of Wheat, margarine or deficit spending.

Although I'd like to think I might have thought up palpating cows. I remember the first time I ran my arm up the back of a cow . . . I discovered a whole new world!

It's enough for me. Alas, I have simple aspirations.

AFTERTHOUGHT

When I consider the inventions that changed my life, I guess it would be the plastic sleeve, insecticide ear tags and the lime squeezer.

ON MOUSTACHE SAFETY

A word about moustache safety and maintenance; HAPHAZARD! There are really no official rules, no regulations passed down. But I suppose one might encounter moustache restrictions for certain jobs like wine tasting, orthodontery, or swallowing fire.

LeeRay sported a Yosemite Sam Moustache. Last calving season he was attacked by a mama cow who plowed a furrow with him 12 feet long in the thick dirt and muck!

"Are you alright?" yelled the cowboys.

LeeRay staggered to his feet. He looked like a 200-pound breaded muskrat! He blinked back the tears and said, "I think I swallowed my moustache!"

AFTERTHOUGHT
I didn't like my beard at first, but then it grew on me.

ON YOUR OWN WORST ENEMY

My friend John was laying himself a nice sandstone floor on his mother-in-law's veranda. He'd bought a new cement-cutting blade for his circular saw. "Doin' it right!" he said to himself.

He started down a line on a piece 4-foot long. Then the blade tied up! He pushed and pushed, eventually cursing the &^$!* sandstone, the veranda, the mother-in-law (under his breath), the blade and the &^$#@ Chinese workers who made this #%&!!!! saw!

His wife heard the racket. She peeked out. "Maybe," she said, "It would cut a little easier if you took your knee off the cord!"

AFTERTHOUGHT

Isn't making a smoking section in the restaurant like making a peeing section in the swimming pool?

ON COFFEE SHOP EXPERTS

Nobody is better at givin' advice than a bunch of fellers sittin' around a table drinkin' coffee. We have opinions on how the neighbor should work his cows, how the president should run the country, how the widow should raise her kids and how the coach should handle the team. Yep, we have all the answers.

Too bad no one ever asks us!

AFTERTHOUGHT
Do Lipton Tea employees take coffee breaks?

ON E HOMINY GRITS

eHarmony.complicate is an internet dating service. They send you a questionnaire to find the perfect match. I was helping one of my cowboy friends to fill it out.

Here's as far as we got:

Do you prefer a woman that is tall or short?
It depends on whether she's shining my boots or sitting in front of me in a theater.

Do you consider yourself an epicurian?
No, I'm mostly a Methodist.

When was the last time you had a tryst with a woman?
Not sure, I was in Heber City a while back and this gal made me some scones.

How do you feel about women who work outside the home?
Long as she has company insurance it's okay with me.

Would you decline dating a woman with prison tattoos?
If my name was spelt right it would be fine.

Do aggressive women turn you off?
It depends on whether she is carrying a concealed weapon.

Have you spent much time around dogs?
Well, if you hook me up again, this will be the third time I've tried to get a date on this website.

Do you like horses?
Shore I do, but I'm lookin' for a girl this time.

What do you consider your strongest feature?
Some have said I have beady eyes, a long nose, a pot belly and body odor. So, I'd have to say body odor.

What is the highest level of education you've achieved?
I got half way through a horse shoeing school so I can only do the front feet!

SOMETIMES YOU ASK YOURSELF, "WHY?"

In an effort to get his kids involved Jeff bought a few cows, a head catch and 7 panels. He wired them together and began.

The kids were waving and hollering trying to drive the cow to the head gate. Jeff was trying to get the bar behind the cow, then race up to the head gate to catch her. It took 20 minutes to catch the first one!

Finally the cow tore the gate off and knocked Dad down! The family watched in awe. Jeff was mad. He mumbled something and the kids froze! The middle child said, "Dad...?"

Jeff looked at his family and the concerned expressions on their faces. He waited for them to say, "...are you alright?...the cow's running away!..your shirt is torn!..."

He waited. "Dad," said the kid, "You said the "S" word!"

AFTERTHOUGHT
What happened to Preparation A through G?

128

Out There

ON THE MIDDLE OF NOWHERE

The more I work with real cowboys, the more I realize how little I know.

Much of a cowboy's life is spent hunting for and observing cows. A much smaller part is what defines them to urban people; western paintings, western museums and the movies.

I appreciate these real cowboys for helpin' me learn their world. It would be nice to be one of them but I fear, I have spent too long in school and not enough time in the middle of nowhere, and it has inhibited my ability to learn the simple things.

I guess it's the price I pay for being funny.

AFTERTHOUGHT
In answer to the question, "Are you a cowboy?" I say I'm a better cowboy poet.

ON DRIVING LESSONS WITH AUNT EFFIE

We'd been to a fiddlin' and she and Uncle Len let me drive home in their 1953 Chevrolet long bed pickup. I was 15.

It was rainin' buckets. The right side windshield wiper quit working! The headlights cut tunnels into the darkness. Aunt Effie was nearly in my lap trying to see out the swiping fan on the left wiper!

She was giving me a "play by play" of our location, "Aunt Effie," I shouted over the pouring rain, "Can you reach the brakes from there?"

"Bax, honey, you know I can't drive! Bear to the right at the top of the hill! I believe that's the Slaughterville road!"

AFTERTHOUGHT
You never really learn to swear until you learn to drive.

ON THE SIMPLE ANSWER

They tell of a crusty ol' coyote-hunting crop-duster in Montana who was teaching flying lessons. One particularly talkative know-it-all student showed up for his 6th lesson. Ol' Montana told him to climb in on the pilot's side, that he was ready to go.

"Gosh," said the student, "I've only had five lessons, most people say you need at least seven, I'm not sure I'm ready. I've read about the danger of flying before your confidence is built up, I'm just concerned we might be jumping the gun, are you sure I'm ready to solo, what if I crash?"

Ol' Monty patted him on the arm and said, "Sonny, this isn't my plane and you're no kin to me, so take your best shot."

AFTERTHOUGHT
He doesn't suffer from insanity . . . he enjoys it!

ON TAKING A LEFT AT CONFUSION

Dally had his map out and was cussing his GPS when he ran the stop sign. The officer listened to his story, "One, I'm lost. Two, I'm confused, and Three, I'm scared because I'm lost and confused!"

"Let me see your license."

In the confusion Dally dropped his wallet and his Concealed Weapons permit. The policeman drew back, "Do you have a weapon on you now?...ever been arrested?" "No, No!" Dally protested.

"Where are you going?"

"Well, depending on where I am, I was hoping to see the shoreline."

"Easy enough. Take a left at Hwy 290. If you miss it, the next shoreline you will see will be in New Jersey!"

AFTERTHOUGHT
He lied like an eye witness.

ON PLANTS FEELING PAIN:
THE VEGETARIAN'S NIGHTMARE

I planted a garden last April
And lovingly sang it a ballad.
But later in June, beneath a full moon,
Forgive me, I wanted a salad!

So I slipped out and fondled a carrot
Caressing its feathery top
With the force of a brute I tore out the root!
It whimpered and came with a pop.

I violated tomatoes
So their innards could never survive.
I grated and ground 'til they made not a sound
Then I boiled the tater alive!

I ate them. Forgive me I'm sorry.
But hear me though I'm a beginner,
Those plants feel pain
Though it's hard to explain
To someone who eats them for dinner!

AFTERTHOUGHT
What did they call Neanderthal vegetarians? Bad Hunters.

134

ON PILLS

I ran into a lady who has a pill for everything! I gave that some thought. What kind of pills would really help me?

Have you ever forgotten to pay your credit card bill? It's too late to avoid that 17% interest on your next bill. But say you had a bottle of "PAY-BACK" capsules that instantly eliminate the penalty.

Have you ever raised your hand at the auction, only to find you are bidding on the wrong animal? You pop a "WHOA, HOLD IT!" pill! Faster than nitroglycerine, it wipes out the last thing you said!

There could be "WHOOPS!" pills, "OVERS!" pills, "WAIT UP!" pills and "IT WAS AN ACCIDENT!" pills for those times you spoke your mind... and shouldn't have. Which happens to me all the time. Pass me a "SILENCER", I'll swallow it whole!

AFTERTHOUGHT
All I want is a meaningful overnight relationship.

ON THE AXIS OF IDEAL UNDERSTANDING

I have developed a way to evaluate when a person reaches the pinnacle of their profession. I call it the "Peak of Practical Intelligence."

It states there is a point in the lifetime of a profession where your dependence on your knowledge derived from Education (ED) equals your dependence on your knowledge gained from Experience (EX).

Thus the lines on the graph will eventually cross. ED will equal EX. That point is your personal Axis of Ideal Understanding. You have reached the Peak of your Practical Intelligence. Thereafter you will rely more on EX than ED.

AFTERTHOUGHT

For my senior paper in vet school I chose the Anatomy of Five Non-Domestic Mammals. The faculty committee threatened to give me a "D" if I chose a subject so frivolous.

I got a "D" but to this day I know that a giraffe has cloven hooves and both the blue whale and elephant have internal testicles.

ON BOTH SIDES OF A TO Z

When I see the letter "A", my mind brings up Anteater; "B" Bag Balm. Deep thinkers would chose Alfresco and Thiamine.

Them: Caviar. Us: Cowpie

D - Department of Defense vs double-wide

E - Entitlement vs eggs and bacon

F - Philosophy vs fishing and flunked English I

G - Government vs gravy

H - Hillary vs Hank the Cowdog

I - International envoy vs International Harvester

J - Jurisprudence vs Judge Judy

K - 401K vs Krispy Kreme

L - Lobbyist vs lotto ticket

M - Meatless Monday vs monkey wrench

N - Nose job vs Nascar

O - Obama vs offsides

P - World Power vs   Poker tournament

R - Regulations vs regular coffee

S - Government service vs drive-in service

T - Tehran vs Trump

U - United Nations vs United States

V - Vice President who? vs Vanna White

W - World Peace vs Hot Wings

X - Xeriscaping vs the spot on the mall map

Y - Yelling at politicians vs Yawning at politicians

Z - Zipping back and forth vs sawing *zzzzzzz*

ON PAT RICHARDSON'S CORRIGIBLES

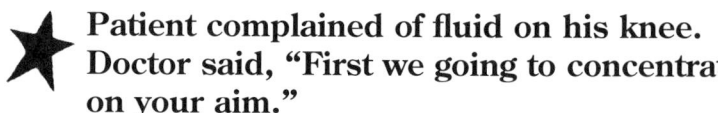 Rodney was being awarded as the best bronc rider to come out of North Dakota. He turned to his wife and said, "Could you ever, in your wildest dreams, believe I would achieve such respect and adoration." She said, "Rodney, you've never been in my wildest dreams."

To help if you're gettin' robbed, yell "FIRE!" instead of "HELP!" unless, of course, he's holding a gun!

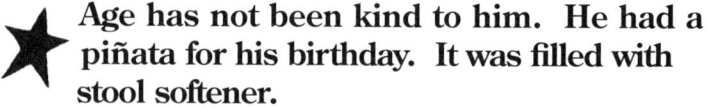 Patient complained of fluid on his knee. Doctor said, "First we going to concentrate on your aim."

Patient had an injured leg and asked Doctor what he should do. Doctor said, "Limp."

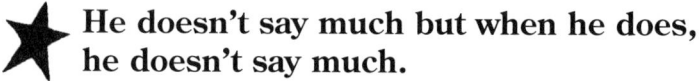 Age has not been kind to him. He had a piñata for his birthday. It was filled with stool softener.

You can't take it with you. You never see a U-Haul trailer on a hearse.

He doesn't say much but when he does, he doesn't say much.

ON TRANSPLANTING BODY PARTS

It is becoming commonplace. Celebrities are always on the look out for transplant donors and insuring their precious body parts.

For instance what if Tiger Woods wants to donate his back swing? or George Strait's teeth, or Willie Nelson's generous offer, "All of me, Why not take all of me..."

I, myself don't have much to offer; A bent thumb, an occasional molar and there's not much market for astigmatism. I guess I've worn out most of my body parts.

So, all I've got that is worth trading is my moustache; maybe I could lease it out on Ground Hog Day...well, just an idea.

AFTERTHOUGHT
I always thought it would take longer to get older! - Steve Radokavich

Flag and Faith

ON SUNDAY HEADED HOME

I've been a travelin' man most of my life as a veterinarian and later as an entertainer. My jobs are on weekends so Sunday means I'm usually on the road and headed home. Most times I'm drivin' a rent car to an airport.

Sunday mornings my spirits are high. The folks that invite me to their town are my folks, country people; God, America and Values. As the camaraderie sinks in, I inevitably talk to God.

He travels with me and Sunday we have a little private time. Which is generous considering all the church services He's committed to! But that doesn't stop me from rattlin' on and, somehow He always seems to have time to listen . . . and I don't take it for granted.

AFTERTHOUGHT

"Hello, Father O'Malley, we need your help. This is the IRS. Is a Ted Houlihan a member of your congregation?"
"He is!"
"Did he donate $10,000 to the church?"
"He will!"

ON THE POWER OF PRAYER

At the time of the NFR in Las Vegas the world was in chaos, terrorism reigned. All Around Champion Trevor Brazile spoke from the award stage. I paraphrase;

He gave thanks to God, said America was built on Christian faith, that we can be merciful and forgiving to others but that does not include forsaking our beliefs just because it offends somebody.

When Lee Greenwood sang "God Bless the USA," the roof came off the auditorium, people wiped their eyes and you could hear it as far away as Tulsa!

AFTERTHOUGHT
It is common in rodeo for a rider or roper to genuflect or point upward after his run...do a Tebow, I guess. We don't mock him...we know who he is talkin' to.

ON COWS IN THE MANGER

What difference does it matter if a cow was in the barn when Jesus was born? To me it gives us livestock people a personal connection.

We can picture the trough that Mary laid the baby Jesus in. Straw in the bottom, a fleece, maybe a saddle blanket to wrap Him.

Jesus was born of regular, decent working-class people. He had a normal life growing up; feeding the stock and doin' his chores. I think God did it so that we, common people might relate to Him more easily. It is humbling to know that the only guests they had that night were shepherds!

AFTERTHOUGHT

For Mary's sake, it's too bad Joe didn't stop along the road a bit earlier that night, like at a farmhouse. But Joe was in a hurry to get to Bethlehem, and you know how men are.

ON CHRISTMAS GIFT EXCHANGES
ON THE FARM

The buzzard drew the possum. He gave him reflector tape for obvious reasons. The dog presented the cat a can full of sand and a gift certificate to be spayed. The cat reciprocated with a toy flea circus for the dog.

By some coincidence the sheep had all drawn each other, and each gave the other a picture of a sheep. Some thought it was a mirror.

The rooster gave the mouse the requisite cheese, the mouse gave the rooster a weekend for two at Campbell's Chicken Noodle Soup Resort. It included a room with a stew.

AFTERTHOUGHT

At the end of the evening the farmer and his wife were given a book autographed by all their cloven hoofed and feathered edible animal friends entitled, "The Vegetarian Cookbook, or How to get the Most out of a Tuber during the Holidays." And, yes they all 'chipped' in.

ON FAITH AND BUSINESS

1) In business Faith can be demonstrated by:

a) Trusting another person is good for his word, b) confidence that a partner or employee will do their part, and c) shooting arrows in the sky to attract business.

2) In moral sensibilities Faith can be demonstrated by:

a) Relying on the promise of another person's love, b) believing there is some good in even the worst miscreant, and c) intuition.

3) In spiritual things Faith is demonstrated by:

a) Charitable giving, b) practicing forgiveness and mercy to all who offend, and c) humility.

AFTERTHOUGHT

A strong Faith is essential in entrepreneurism. You must believe in yourself. If you have already developed the ability to have faith by believing in God, then believing in your aspirations comes easy.

ON MEMORIAL DAY

My thoughts go back to a friend from college, Clovis May. Drafted December 1967.

Those of us who stayed home and watched the reception of our returning soldiers, our fellow Americans, get smeared, cursed, and reviled by a heartless, gutless group of protesters...we who watched and said nothing shamed ourselves by letting their hatred go unanswered.

If America owes anyone an apology, Vietnam Vets are at the top of the list.

AFTERTHOUGHT
Sgt. Clovis Lee May, Infantry, US Army
Dec 14, 1944 - May 22, 1969
Killed in Action

THANKSGIVING THOUGHTS

Not everyone has a car, owns a home, carries a cell phone, knows who the 18th president is and can hum "Blue Eyes Cryin' in the Rain."

But everyday, three times a day, every person eats something you farmers produce. You are more essential to their lives than their bookie, their broker, their drug dealer, their teacher, their boss, or even...their best friend!

Do those of you who farm and ranch think about the lives you touch? J.K. Rowling sold 450 million Harry Potter books! Wow! 114 million watched the Super Bowl! Double Wow!

You set the table for 325,944,738 Americans ...everyday...three times a day. So this Thanksgiving we thank the Lord and express our appreciation to you farmers and ranchers for keeping America's food plentiful and safe, and the hundreds of millions of us fed.

Pass the cranberries please.

AFTERTHOUGHT
Why do croutons come in airtight packages? Aren't they just stale bread to begin with?

DOES KINDNESS MATTER

A gentleman at a traffic stop in New Mexico was approached by a homeless man. The driver tried to wave the panhandler away but he shook his head and pointed to the front bumper.

The driver rolled his window down and heard the homeless say, "No! I have something for you. Your license about supporting cancer relief...I had lung cancer. I'm alive because of them!"

Then he pulled out a wrinkled dollar bill and gave it to the driver.

Hope, where it wasn't expected.

AFTERTHOUGHT
The book "Who Really Cares," by Arthur Brooks (2006) analyzes "the practice of donating both time and/or money to "worthy causes," ranks those who regularly attend church as the most generous contributors.

HORSE LOVER'S CHRISTMAS

One of the most difficult questions every Christmas for Horse Lovers is what to get for that family member that brings you the most joy...And I don't mean your dog.

Christmas shopping for a dog is easy; something to chew on, for a cat; something to play with, for a python; something to squeeze.

But a horse would rather that you got something for yourself; new chaps, jodhpurs, a hat, boots, saddle or braided reins. That's how your horse thinks. He wants you to look good, to feel pretty and to shine.

People could learn a lot from horses.

AFTERTHOUGHT
You can talk to your horse for 30 minutes and they'll listen patiently. They care. You can lean on a horse. Try leaning on a cat.

ON CONSOLATION

In life, grown children often take the responsibility for their parents when they get old. It is a task done out of love and responsibility.

But in real life we know that old age changes people. The caregiver watches them change into someone we don't know. We grit our teeth and forge on and often sleep with them to keep them safe from themselves through the night.

We steel our emotions, concentrate on the mundane and perform the tasks required. It is frustrating, exhausting and heart-wrenching.

But when the time comes, feelings that have taken their toll on our compassion will disappear overnight. Take comfort in knowing that the difficult person you have been caring for, is not the same person that will live on in your heart.

AFTERTHOUGHT

Exodus 20:12 Honor your father and your mother, that your days may be long upon the land which the Lord your God is giving you.

ON THE TEN PERCENT

Ten percent of the people
do 90% of the work
And they get to do it for nothin'!
And that's not the only perk,

They're asked to donate to causes,
contribute their cash and their time
Get up early, usually stay late,
and always claim they don't mind.

The ten percent you can count on
to sign up, to help and belong
Always ready and willing,
they make our communities strong.

What causes man to serve his fellow man?
At best, I discern
Not money, Sometimes a 'thanks'
is all that they'll earn.

No physical exam can spot it,
it won't show up on the chart
But if I had to guess what IT is,
I'd say it comes from the heart.

So, I'll just admit that we're lucky
the ten percent are right here
'Cause without them nothing would happen,
and they do it all volunteer.

VOL from the Greek meaning; work like a horse
UNTEER meaning; without pay

Riding Drag

ON PLAY LIKE I'M NOT HERE

A cowboy magazine photographer, named Simington, discussed with Dave what he was hoping to capture on film, "You guys do what you normally do, just play like I'm not here."

Somewhere along the way Simington's horse had enough of the off-balance, jaw-jerkin', foot slappin', click-clackin', snappin' slow-stoppin', jerk-jabbin' orangutan on his back!

Dave said it was painful to watch. Simington was ejected out into space! With all his accoutrements, in mid air he looked like a satellite spreading its solar panels!

"What did you do?" I asked Dave.

"Well," he said, "He crashed, rolled over and went to pickin' up the pieces of his stuff so... I just rode on by...and played like he wasn't there."

AFTERTHOUGHT
You're never too old to learn something stupid.

ON CAMPING IN WYOMING

Roy was proud of his new light-weight polyester tent. Regina smiled nervously. He put the new wood burning camp stove between their cots and dozed off peacefully. Regina felt the wind rising. Suddenly the new tent spread it wings and she was looking up at the starry sky!

Behind her, the portable stove took a deep breath and set the tent on fire! Roy jumped up clad in his skivvies and attacked it with bottles of water and cans of beer; racing back and forth in front of the blaze.

He minced and pirouetted, hopping and whooping like an Arapahoe brave with Tourette's Syndrome! Finally he dumped the cooler on the fire!

As they recalled the story at breakfast next morning, someone mentioned Kevin Costner.

"Costner?" asked Roy. "Yeah, Dances With Flames."

AFTERTHOUGHT
Horace Greeley said, "Go west young man!" and 300 people in San Francisco drowned.

ON THE ART OF DRIVING THE SON

My son has been driving since he was ten; jeeps, tractors, trucks, etc. Then came the time for the HOLY GRAIL...the driver's license test! He borrowed Mom's Buick Submarine.

He flunked two days in a row because he couldn't back into a perpendicular parking spot! He kept at it and on the second test day he backed into a tree!

We finally borrowed a neighbor's smaller car and he passed the test! On the way home he was jubilant! Mom suggested that he gas up the neighbor's car as a way to thank her. He inserted the nozzle, ran into the store for a Monster pop, returned, jumped behind the wheel and took off...ripping the gasoline hose off at the pump.

AFTERTHOUGHT

It took four weeks to pay the $72 bill to repair the hose. I think he learned a lesson...but I'm not sure.

ON MY PERSONAL BEST

One summer I was cited for going too slow in California and for going too fast in Texas.

The same winter in northern New Mexico I was cited for passing a policeman on a double-yellow line.

I, also, am the first person to receive a traffic ticket on Peña Boulevard. It is the freeway from Denver to the Denver International Airport and ...I was cited for speeding between El Paso and Alamagordo twice...two days in a row, going and coming!

I could include incidences like walking down the center rail on I-25 from Evans to S. Broadway at 10pm or being "officially detained" by sheriff's deputies in the Orange County airport for molesting a stamp machine.

Ah, days to remember...

AFTERTHOUGHT
You don't need a parachute to sky dive. You only need a parachute if you're planning to sky dive twice.

ON ANIMAL NAMING ABUSE

"Common language on fauna betrays an anthropocentric bias. Words such as 'pets' 'wildlife' and 'vermin' are derogatory..." says director of the Oxford Center for Animal Ethics.

Even using similes like 'sly as a fox', 'drunk as a skunk' and 'perky as a porpoise,' are considered animal abuse. Actually the word 'Animal' is not approved. The description 'Differentiated Being' is preferred. FRIGHTENING!

It's nice to know there are other people who think outside the box. Civilization needs them to help us define the difference between normal and hallucinatory. The director illustrates my point and, forgive my anthropomorphic bias, is crazy as a loon!

AFTERTHOUGHT
I wonder how many roadkills are suicides?

THE LEGEND OF BAD GUYS

The West was peppered with bad guys
whose conduct was misunderstood
Yet, today we treat them as heroes
like they were a Robin Hood.

We tend to portray them as victims,
who through no fault of their own
Grew up to be convicts and perverts, but,
hey, they were raised in a broken home.

They'd rob from the wealthy it's storied.
They'd plunder and steal for a lark.
Then pass out gift boxes on weekends
to orphans and nuns in the park.

They'd burn down a village but were sorry,
and regretted things even worse.
Darlin' Nell got caught in the cross fire, they
cried as they lifted her purse.

They never intended to hurt folks,
but accidents happen, they do!
Now we speak of them all with compassion,
'cause bad guys have feelings, too.

We sing of their legends in ballads,
we lift up their deeds in a song
And although it sounds so romantic,
to me it seems dreadfully wrong.

'Cause Pancho Villa was a narcisstic bag of
sheep pellets. So was Billy the Kid.
Jessie James became a hero for the foul,
evil deeds that he did.

The Bandit Joaquin was a horse thief,
Claude Dallas a cowardly swain,
The Sundance Kid was a scumbag
who got his thrill robbin' the train.

The Godfather made folks an offer
he said they couldn't refuse
If they did he'd take them out swimming,
wearing their concrete shoes

Bonnie and Clyde were both psychos,
Pretty Boy Floyd was a rat
And Pancho Villa was a narcisstic bag of
sheep pellets, but I guess I done told you that.

ON LIZARD ABUSE

HEADLINE May 1, 2038

Xtreme HSUS Files Suit Against Geico For Lizard Abuse

"It's a long time coming," said Sue Sly, Exec Dir. "After we protected horses, eliminated factory farming, outlawed fishing, interspecies cow milking, aquariums and animal crackers, reptile protection was obvious."

"Will the courts hear your case," asked the reporter, "because everybody knows the lizard in the commercial is not real?"

"All we have to prove is the 'illusion' of abuse and mistreatment."

OFF THE RECORD
"But the lizard isn't real." "Kids don't know that," said Sly. "They grow into adults who don't know!"

AFTERTHOUGHT
Do you like sushi? We used to call it bait.

160

ON CLEANING UP YOUR MESS

Ask yourself, "Do you make messes or clean them up?"

In this time of protesting, marching, window smashing, looting, foul graffiti, burning buildings, dissing school faculty and political mud throwing all being done in the name of a cause...Who cleans up the day after?

Obviously many think it is their right to vandalize, threaten, burn, bomb, steal and throw sand in anybody's gas tank...as long as your cause is righteous.

But we know who cleans up after them, don't we; the garbage crews, nurses, social workers, construction people, sweepers, undertakers, hospital caretakers, policemen, auto mechanics, body shops, et. al. People that the protesters and marchers wouldn't "give the time of day."

How about half of the sign-carriers bring a broom and trash can? That couldn't be too much to ask.

Maybe someone would take you seriously.

AFTERTHOUGHT
Another case of the haves vs the have-nots.

ON GOOD DEEDS GONE AWRY

Scott explained his story. An elderly lady came down the aisle with her walker, squeezed over and sat down beside him.

Scott said the lady was nice and laughed a lot. When the show was over she stood to leave, then tottered and seemed to collapse!

Scott caught her. She was so light, so frail, he remembered. She said something he didn't catch and then toppled over again! Once more he stepped in to save the day!

"Why don't you just sit down and I'll go get your walker," Scott offered.

She turned to look at him and said, "I was trying to tell you, sonny, the usher's got my walker and is waiting for me. And if you'll just let me pick up my purse, I'll go!"

AFTERTHOUGHT
On the way here I found out the shortest distance between two points is under construction.

ON BAXTER BLACK

Baxter Black has spent his life serving the people who make their living 'off the land', from the littlest shepherd to the most prestigious seed soil scientist. They are part of his world. From shoeing a horse, ridin' pens, pulling calves, riding bulls, shearing ewes, rotating pastures, diagnosing disease, explaining physiology, making you laugh and, most of all, helping you feel proud of what we do...feed the world. Of course, the 'cowboy' in his stories are always the butt of the joke. After all, it's the truth in humor that makes it funny...that's why there are no science fiction jokes.

ON BOB BLACK

Bob was always a little slow. At 70, still waiting for his voice to change, he sits in the principal's office and begs not to be held back in the 3rd grade for yet another year. Principal Dawson muses, noting that Bob has mis-spelled his own name on his last exam...it's a tough call.

Bob lives in Arizona with his beautiful wife and sneezes for a living.

ON CHARLIE MARSH

Charlie, at a recent family reunion, was talking to two new generation art students who promptly whipped out iphones and showed him their latest works -- all done on computer. He didn't have an iphone so couldn't show them anything. He explained that he drew with a pencil (blank looks all around) which he did have with him. They studied it with amazement but soon handed it back, unable to turn it on. Yes, time has moved on, leaving Charlie, his wife, Pat, assorted dogs, cats and cows stranded on small patch in Briartown, Oklahoma.

ON ETIENNE ETCHEVERRY

A second-generation Basque-American, raised in West Texas and southeastern New Mexico and educated at New Mexico State University.

In 60 plus years, A-10 has been a cowboy, a potash miner, a trucker, a professional student and a school teacher. He currently resides in Truth or Consequences, New Mexico. He received the Academy of Western Artists Award in 1998 for cowboy cartoonist of the year. He is always searching for a new story that will turn into one of his cartoons.